HORRORGAMI

25 Creepy Creatures, Ghastly Ghouls, and Other Fiendish Paper Projects

chris mark~

RUNNING PRESS
PHILADELPHIA • LONDON

First published in the United States in 2012 by Running Press Book Publishers
A Member of the Perseus Books Group

Books published by Running Press are available at special discounts for bulk purchases in the
United States by corporations, institutions, and other organizations. For more information,
please contact the Special Markets Department at the Perseus Books Group, 2300 Chestnut
Street, Suite 200, Philadelphia, PA 19103, or call (800) 810-4145, ext. 5000, or e-mail special.
markets@perseusbooks.com.

ISBN 978-0-7624-4539-4
Library of Congress Control Number: 2012931363

E-book ISBN 978-0-7624-4733-6

9 8 7 6 5 4 3 2 1
Digit on the right indicates the number of this printing

This book was conceived, designed, and produced
by Paperwasp, an imprint of Balley Design Limited,
The Mews, 16 Wilbury Grove,
Hove, East Sussex, UK, BN3 3JQ
www.paperwaspbooks.com

Creative director: Simon Balley
Designer: Ginny Zeal
Project editor: Kathy Steer
Illustrations: Michelle Tilly

Running Press Book Publishers
2300 Chestnut Street
Philadelphia, PA 19103-4371

Visit us on the web!
www.runningpress.com

Contents

Introduction

Bet you thought origami was all about a calm mind and sending messages of peace and order in the universe—1000 cranes and so on, right? It doesn't have to be like that—welcome to *Horrorgami*, a new, exciting and, most of all, dark way to look at the gentle art of paper folding: more voodoo than how-to.

By bending the normal folding techniques of origami to your evil will, you can make ghoulies, ghosties, and beasties enough to scare your friends witless, hex your enemies, or just theme a totally gruesome Halloween party.

When you try out the models in *Horrorgami*, use your imagination to see what new types of scary folds you can design. You will find it easiest to start at the beginning of the book, working your way through the projects one by one, as some of the models and procedures in later sections are based partially on previous ones. But, if you are an experienced paper folder and can follow origami instructions without too much difficulty, feel free to choose any design as a starting point. Don't worry if you have problems with your initial attempts.

Revisit the instructions and check the illustrations in sequence. At each step, look at the next illustration to see what shape your paper should make as the result of the step you are following. Also remember that the arrows show the direction in which the paper has to be folded. So look very carefully to see which way the arrows go over, through, and under, and fold your paper accordingly. To help you become accomplished at *Horrorgami*, here are some useful tips:

- Fold on a flat surface, such as a tray, table, or book.
- Make your folds neat and accurate. Crease your folds into place by running your thumbnail along them.
- In the illustrations, the shading represents the colored (printed) side of the paper.
- If your origami project isn't working, take some time out. Place the model to one side, go for a walk, have a cup of coffee, or chat with your local Werewolf. Once you are calm, try making a new creation.
- Most of the projects can be folded from one square of paper, but a few require more. The models' introductory instructions clearly state what you will need. If you are using your own paper rather than the paper supplied with this book, make sure it is cut absolutely square. There is nothing more frustrating than trying to fold a nearly square square!
- Regarding paper choices, go for sickly shades to produce convincing skulls, skeletons, witches, and any other hideous apparitions that throng the dark side of your mind.
- Evil cackling while you fold, although not compulsory, will help you get into a suitably maleficent mood.
- Finally, I do hope that you have a fangtastic time folding origami creatures that quench your evil thirst!

Chris Marks

The Fiendish Symbols

The following symbols help explain how Horrorgami's projects are constructed. Make sure that you understand the differences between each fold. If you get them mixed up, there are no guarantees as to what kind of hideous apparitions will appear!

A valley fold (fold toward you, or in front) is indicated by a line of dashes and a solid arrow showing the direction in which the paper has to be folded.

A mountain fold (fold backward, or behind) is indicated by a line of dots and dashes and a hollow-headed arrow showing the direction in which the paper has to be folded.

An arrow which comes back on itself indicates to fold, press flat, and unfold the paper back to its previous position.

A looped arrow indicates to turn the paper over in the direction shown.

Two circling arrows indicate to turn the paper around into the position shown.

A hollow arrow with a short indented tail indicates to open, and press the paper down flat into the position shown in the next illustration.

A hollow arrow with a long tail indicates to pull the paper in the direction shown.

A solid-headed arrow indicates to push the paper in along the fold-lines, as shown.

A swollen arrow with a pointed tail indicates that the illustration alongside is drawn to a larger scale.

A zigzagged arrow drawn on top of the illustration indicates to fold the paper in the direction shown by the arrow. A step fold is made by pleating the paper in a valley and mountain fold.

An arrow with the tail broken near the head indicates to insert the point in to the pocket or underneath the flap of paper as shown.

An arrow with a series of loops in its tail drawn on top of the illustration indicates to roll up the paper in the direction shown by the arrow.

A line with a Z-shape in the middle indicates that there's more paper beyond this point, but it has not been drawn.

A pair of scissors and a solid line indicates to cut the paper. The solid line shows the position of the cut.

A pair of scissors and shaded area indicates to cut away and discard the shaded parts.

A model's difficulty is explained by the following rat symbols:

One rat—easy;

Two rats—medium;

Three rats—difficult;

Four rats—fiendish.

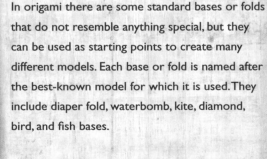

In origami there are some standard bases or folds that do not resemble anything special, but they can be used as starting points to create many different models. Each base or fold is named after the best-known model for which it is used. They include diaper fold, waterbomb, kite, diamond, bird, and fish bases.

Friendly Ghost

This spooky figure loves to hang out around dark and mysterious places—like in the cupboard or in your dusty attic.

you will need:
● Square of paper, white on both sides

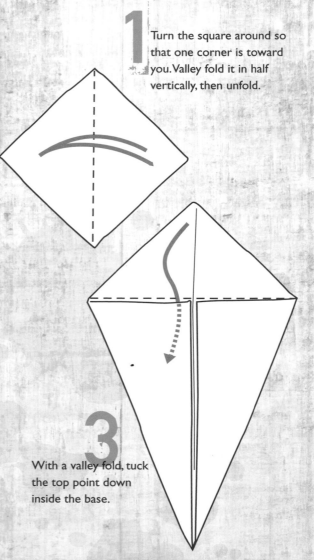

1 Turn the square around so that one corner is toward you. Valley fold it in half vertically, then unfold.

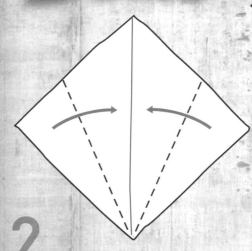

2 From the bottom corner, valley fold the sloping edges in to meet the vertical fold line, making a kite base.

3 With a valley fold, tuck the top point down inside the base.

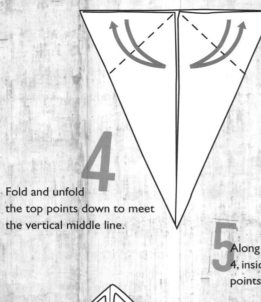

4

Fold and unfold the top points down to meet the vertical middle line.

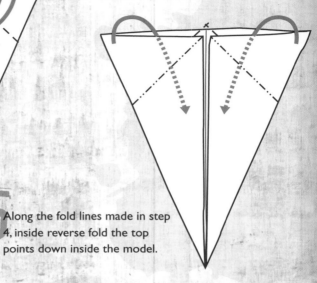

5

Along the fold lines made in step 4, inside reverse fold the top points down inside the model.

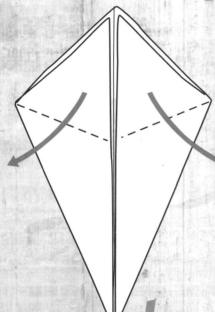

6

Valley fold the two top points down and out to either side.

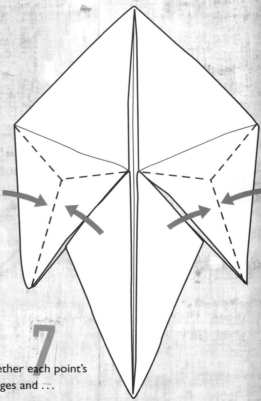

7

Pinch together each point's sloping edges and . . .

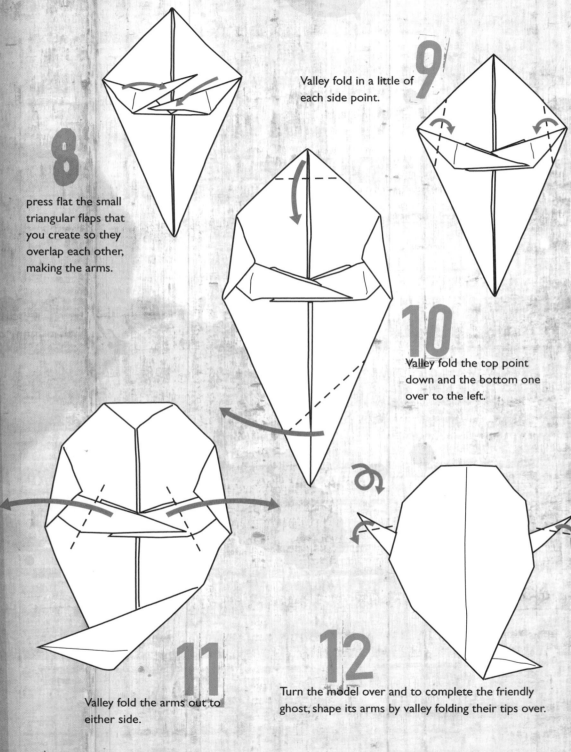

8 press flat the small triangular flaps that you create so they overlap each other, making the arms.

9 Valley fold in a little of each side point.

10 Valley fold the top point down and the bottom one over to the left.

11 Valley fold the arms out to either side.

12 Turn the model over and to complete the friendly ghost, shape its arms by valley folding their tips over.

Draw on my ghostly features and I will come alive!

"Of all ghosts, the ghosts of our old loves are the worst."
Arthur Conan Doyle

Scare Some Jumping Bug

This hair-raising action creature of the night will give the trick or treaters a spook and smile.

you will need:

- Square of paper, plain on one side and colored on the other
- Scissors
- Glue stick
- Medium-size elastic band

1 Cut the square in half horizontally, making two rectangles.

2 Turn one rectangle horizontally, plain side up. From one side begin to tightly roll it up into a firm cylinder . . .

3 and hold it in place with the help of a little glue.

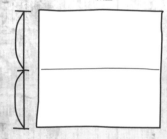

4 Repeat steps 2 and 3 with the remaining rectangle. Let the glue dry.

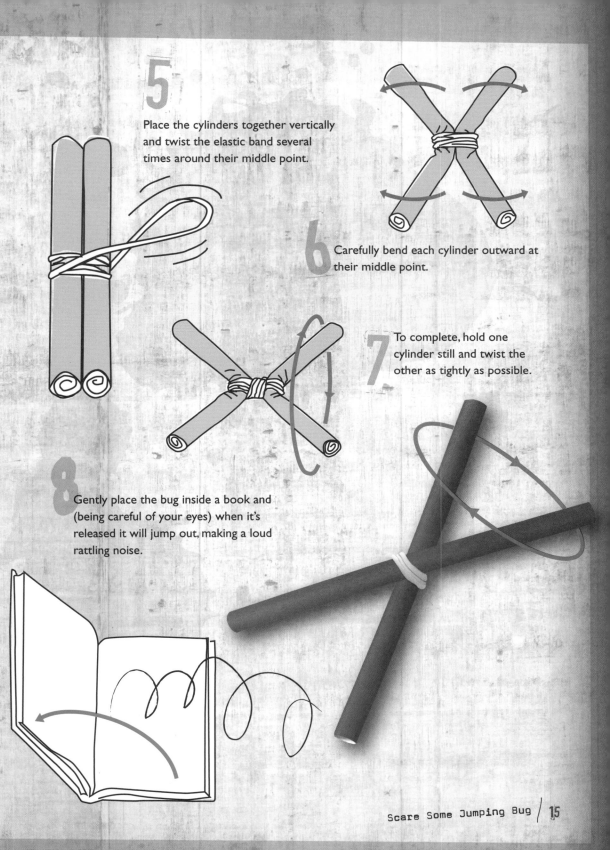

5 Place the cylinders together vertically and twist the elastic band several times around their middle point.

6 Carefully bend each cylinder outward at their middle point.

7 To complete, hold one cylinder still and twist the other as tightly as possible.

8 Gently place the bug inside a book and (being careful of your eyes) when it's released it will jump out, making a loud rattling noise.

Jack-o'-Lantern & Hat

Will this eye-catching Halloween decoration put smiles on the faces of the neighborhood children? His friendly grin and tempting marshmallow treats are sure to leave them asking for some more.

you will need:

- Three squares of paper, identical in size, plain on one side and colored on the other
- Scissors
- Glue stick

1 From one square, cut out a square for the mouth to the size shown.

2 **Lantern:** Fold and unfold one square in half from corner to corner, plain side up.

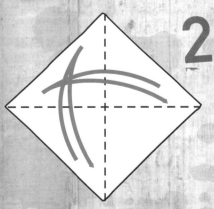

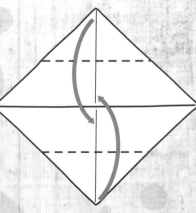

3 Valley fold the top and bottom corners in so that they overlap the middle slightly.

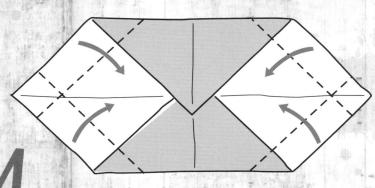

4 Valley fold the top and bottom right- and left-hand sloping edges over as shown.

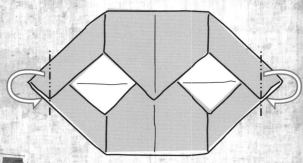

5 To complete, mountain fold the right- and left-hand points behind a little.

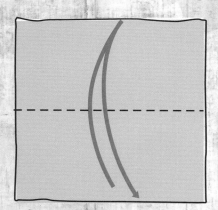

6 **Mouth:** Valley fold the mouth's square in half horizontally, colored side up, then unfold.

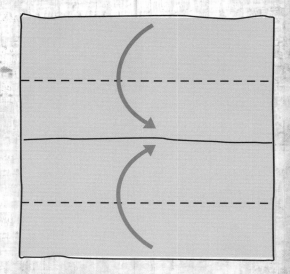

7 Valley fold the top and bottom edges in to meet the horizontal fold line.

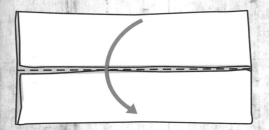

8

Valley fold in half from top to bottom.

9

Mountain fold the bottom right- and left-hand corners up inside the model. Repeat behind.

10

Cut away and discard the shaded part as shown, making a toothy grin.

11

Glue the mouth onto the lantern's lower part as shown.

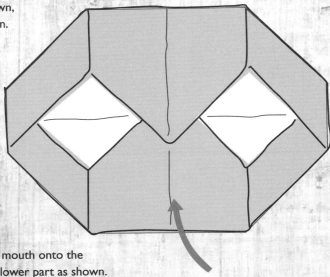

12 Hat: Turn the remaining square around so that one corner is toward you, plain side up. Valley fold it in half horizontally from bottom to top, making a diaper fold.

13 From the top point, valley fold the right-hand sloping edge over to a point one-third of the way across the diaper fold. Repeat with the left-hand sloping edge so that it lies on top.

14 Valley fold the bottom points up as shown.

15 Mountain fold the right- and left-hand points behind.

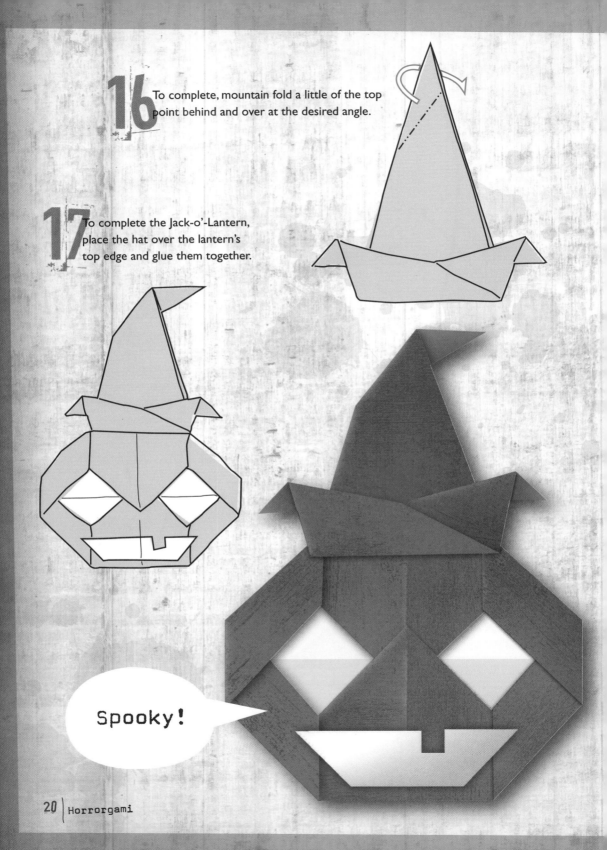

16 To complete, mountain fold a little of the top point behind and over at the desired angle.

17 To complete the Jack-o'-Lantern, place the hat over the lantern's top edge and glue them together.

Spooky!

Flying Evil Witch

This menacing matriarch of the skies, with her evil cackling laugh, is guaranteed to give anyone she encounters an unhealthy drink of revolting spider and toad juice.

you will need:
- Three squares of paper, identical in size, plain on one side and colored on the other
- Scissors
- Glue stick

1

From two squares, cut out squares for the face, hat, and cloak to the size shown.

2

Broomstick: Begin by repeating steps 1 and 2 of the Friendly Ghost on page 10, with the remaining square, plain side up. Stopping short of the bottom point, valley fold the sloping edges over toward the vertical middle line as shown.

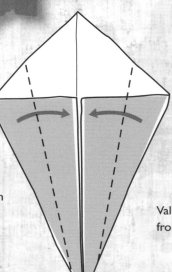

3

Valley fold in half from bottom to top.

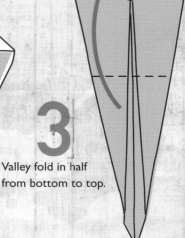

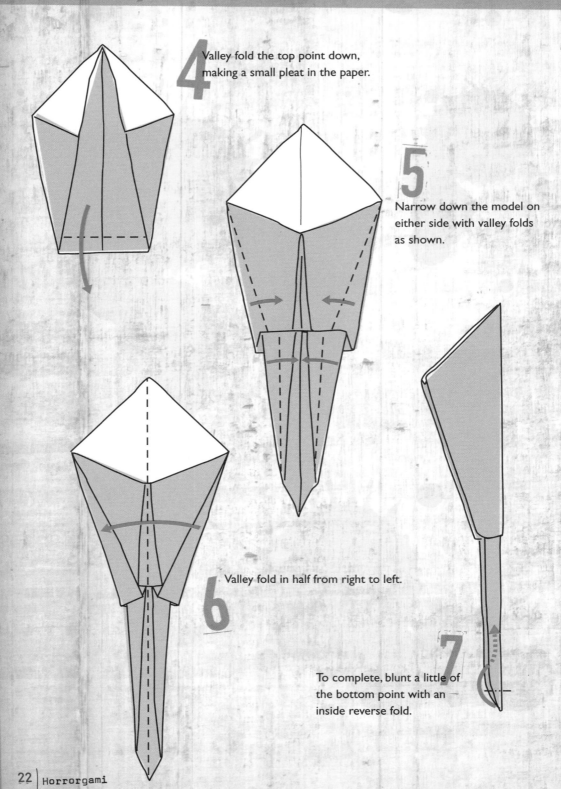

4 Valley fold the top point down, making a small pleat in the paper.

5 Narrow down the model on either side with valley folds as shown.

6 Valley fold in half from right to left.

7 To complete, blunt a little of the bottom point with an inside reverse fold.

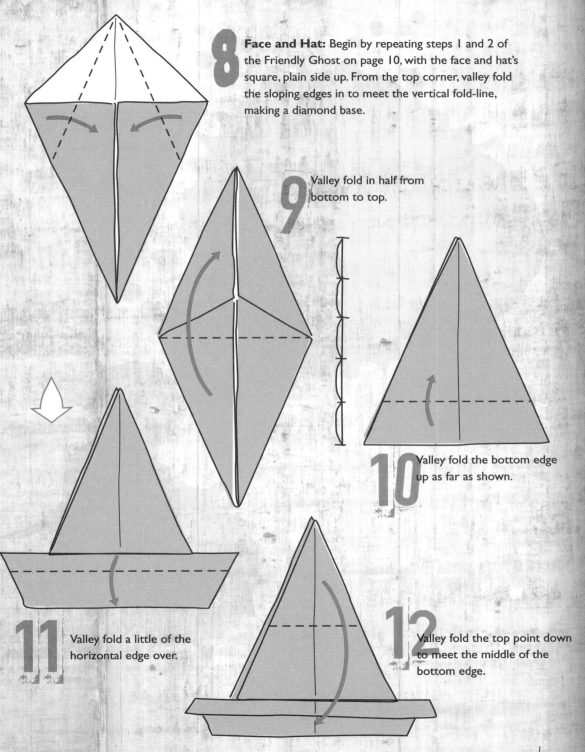

8 **Face and Hat:** Begin by repeating steps 1 and 2 of the Friendly Ghost on page 10, with the face and hat's square, plain side up. From the top corner, valley fold the sloping edges in to meet the vertical fold-line, making a diamond base.

9 Valley fold in half from bottom to top.

10 Valley fold the bottom edge up as far as shown.

11 Valley fold a little of the horizontal edge over.

12 Valley fold the top point down to meet the middle of the bottom edge.

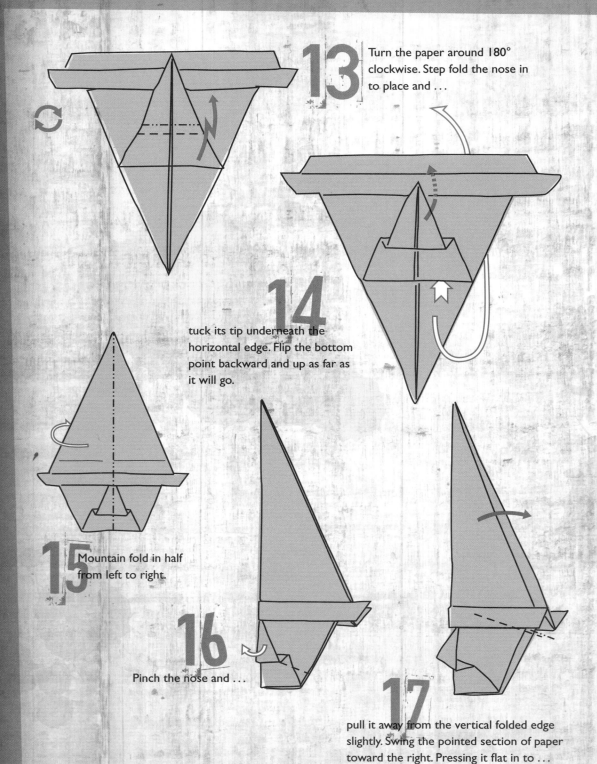

13 Turn the paper around 180° clockwise. Step fold the nose in to place and . . .

14 tuck its tip underneath the horizontal edge. Flip the bottom point backward and up as far as it will go.

15 Mountain fold in half from left to right.

16 Pinch the nose and . . .

17 pull it away from the vertical folded edge slightly. Swing the pointed section of paper toward the right. Pressing it flat in to . . .

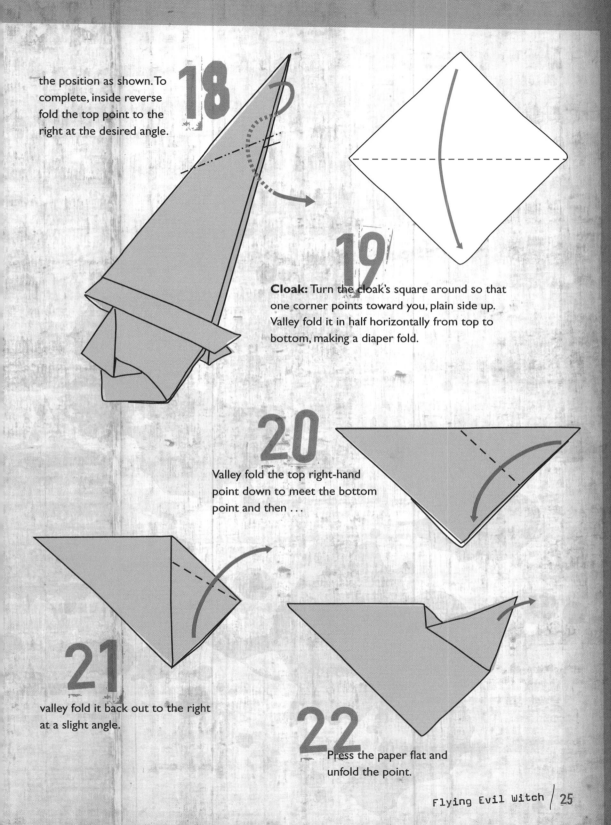

the position as shown. To complete, inside reverse fold the top point to the right at the desired angle.

18

19

Cloak: Turn the cloak's square around so that one corner points toward you, plain side up. Valley fold it in half horizontally from top to bottom, making a diaper fold.

20

Valley fold the top right-hand point down to meet the bottom point and then ...

21

valley fold it back out to the right at a slight angle.

22

Press the paper flat and unfold the point.

23 Along the fold-lines made in steps 20 and 21, step fold the right-hand point on either side down inside the model.

24 To complete, blunt a little of the left-hand point with an inside reverse fold.

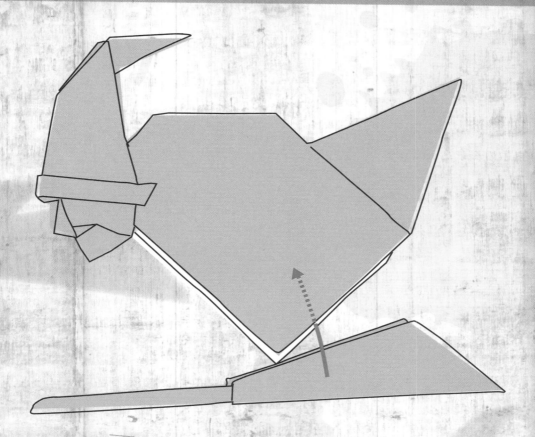

25 To complete the Flying Evil Witch, slip the face and hat over the cloak's blunted point. Insert the broomstick in between the cloak's lower layers at the desired angle. Glue all parts together.

> **"Double, double**
> **toil and trouble,**
> **Fire burn, and cauldron bubble"**
>
> Three Witches, *Macbeth*, Shakespeare

Evil Witch's Cat

When placed on a table or doorstep, this devilish looking cat will give a hair-raising greeting and is sure to thrill any little monsters who visit your gloomy old mansion.

you will need:
- Two squares of paper, identical in size, plain on one side and colored on the other
- Scissors
- Glue stick

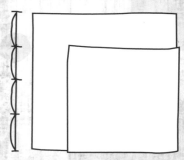

1 From one square, cut out a square for the cat's head to the size shown.

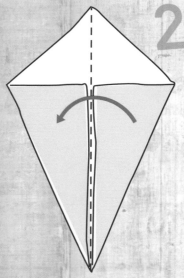

2 **Body:** Begin by repeating steps 1 and 2 of the Friendly Ghost on page 10, with the remaining square, plain side up. Valley fold it in half from right to left.

3 Inside reverse fold the bottom point up in to the position shown by the dotted lines and then . . .

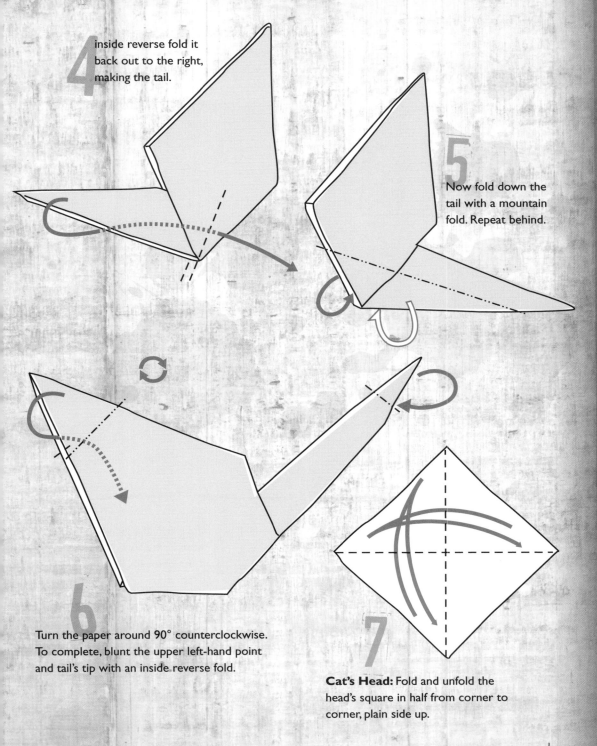

4 inside reverse fold it back out to the right, making the tail.

5 Now fold down the tail with a mountain fold. Repeat behind.

6 Turn the paper around 90° counterclockwise. To complete, blunt the upper left-hand point and tail's tip with an inside reverse fold.

7 **Cat's Head:** Fold and unfold the head's square in half from corner to corner, plain side up.

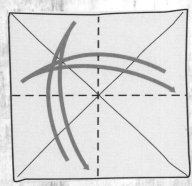

8 Turn the square over and around 90° clockwise. Fold and unfold it in half from side to side and top to bottom.

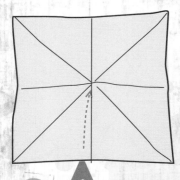

9 From below, push up on the square at its middle point so that the diagonal folds in the paper will flex gently, becoming convex.

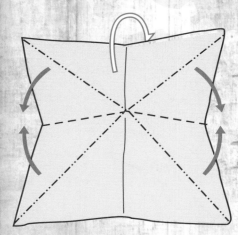

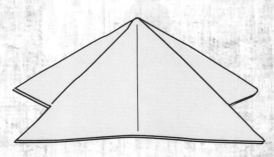

10 Now, using the existing fold-lines, carefully collapse the paper down in to . . .

11 the shape of a pyramid, making a waterbomb base. Make sure that it has two flaps of paper on either side.

12 Valley fold the right- and left-hand points up to meet the top point and then . . .

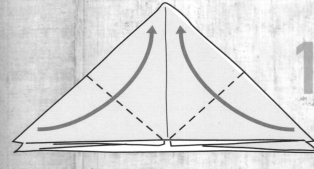

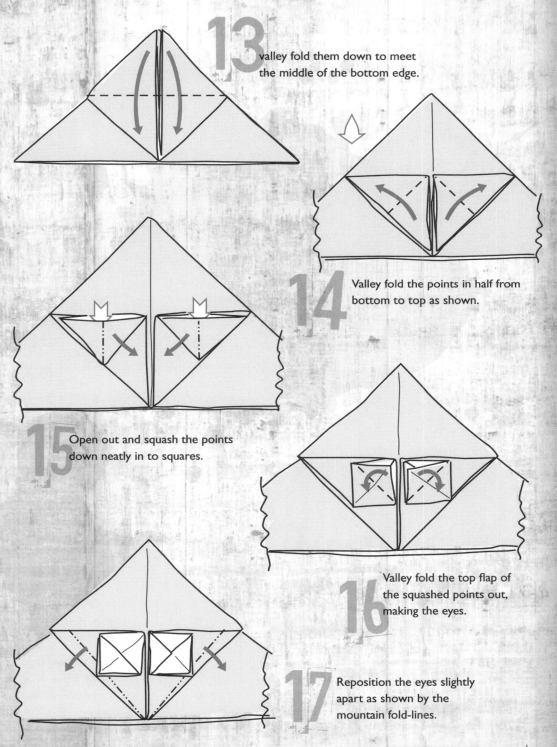

13 valley fold them down to meet the middle of the bottom edge.

14 Valley fold the points in half from bottom to top as shown.

15 Open out and squash the points down neatly in to squares.

16 Valley fold the top flap of the squashed points out, making the eyes.

17 Reposition the eyes slightly apart as shown by the mountain fold-lines.

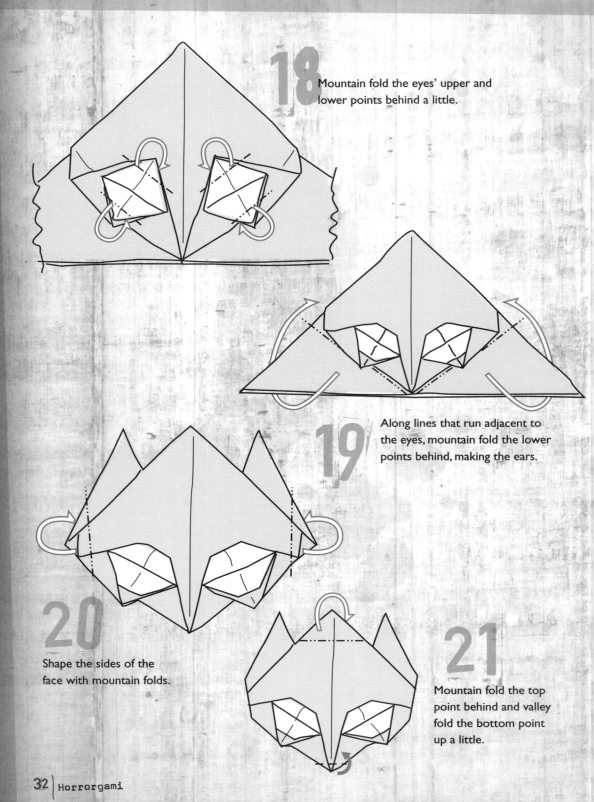

18 Mountain fold the eyes' upper and lower points behind a little.

19 Along lines that run adjacent to the eyes, mountain fold the lower points behind, making the ears.

20 Shape the sides of the face with mountain folds.

21 Mountain fold the top point behind and valley fold the bottom point up a little.

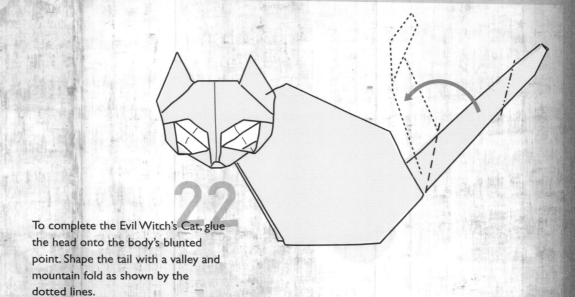

To complete the Evil Witch's Cat, glue the head onto the body's blunted point. Shape the tail with a valley and mountain fold as shown by the dotted lines.

Meow!
Meow!

Beastly Bat

Go batty and have spooktacular fun as you conjure up fiendish miniature bats to live in a crumbling brick ruin. Why not hang life-size versions in your doorway to greet visitors face to face?

you will need:

● Square of paper, plain on one side and colored on the other

● Scissors

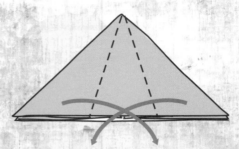

1 Begin by repeating steps 7 to 11 of the Evil Witch's Cat on page 28, with the square. From the top point, valley fold the right-hand sloping edge over to a point one-third of the way across the base. Repeat with the left-hand sloping edge so that it lies on top.

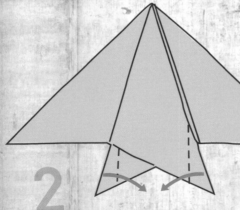

2 Valley fold each of the bottom points inward a little, making the legs.

3 Cut away and discard the shaded parts as shown, making the ears.

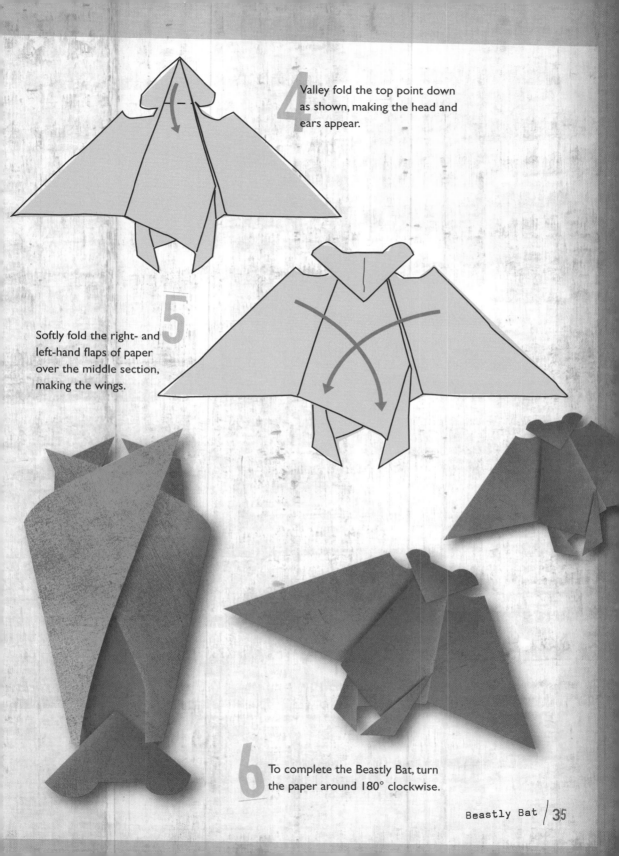

4 Valley fold the top point down as shown, making the head and ears appear.

5 Softly fold the right- and left-hand flaps of paper over the middle section, making the wings.

6 To complete the Beastly Bat, turn the paper around 180° clockwise.

Hooded Grim Reaper

This hood-cloaked, scythe-wielding figure is the personification of death. We all know exactly who he is and what he wants. He comes for every person, hourglass in hand, waiting for the last grain of sand to fall.

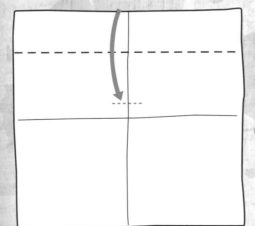

you will need:
- Square of paper, plain on one side and colored on the other

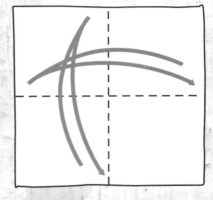

1 Fold and unfold the square in half from side to side and top to bottom, plain side up.

2 Stopping slightly short of the middle, valley fold the top edge down as shown.

Angel of Death!

3

Mountain fold the top corners behind to meet the vertical fold-line.

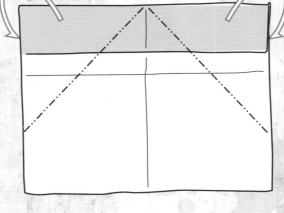

4

Valley fold the right- and left-hand sides in on a slant so that their upper points meet the vertical fold-line as shown.

5

Valley fold in half from right to left, while at the same time letting the triangular section of paper rise up.

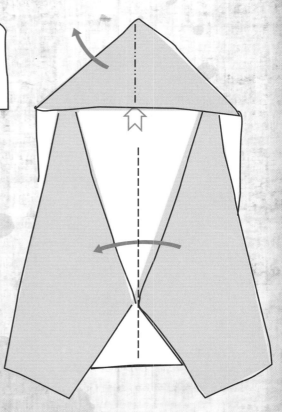

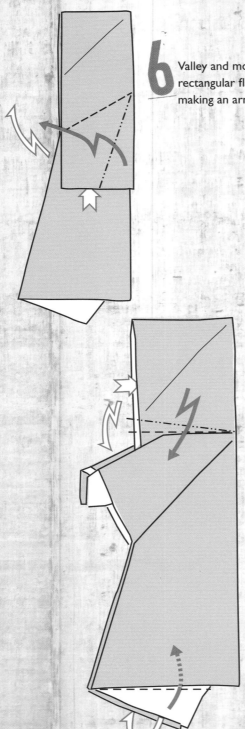

6 Valley and mountain fold the front rectangular flap of paper upward, making an arm. Repeat behind.

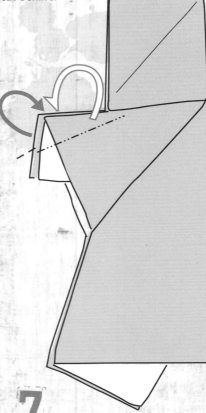

7 Shape the arm with a mountain fold. Repeat behind.

8 Step fold the upper section of paper on either side as shown. Valley fold the bottom triangular flap of paper up inside the model. Repeat behind.

What's happening, dude?

Death is upon us!

"You can be a king or a street sweeper, but everybody dances with the Grim Reaper"
Robert Alton Harris

Reaper's Scythe

The Grim Reaper's job is to help people face their own death and he is most commonly pictured with a scythe, a tool used for harvesting crops and mowing grass. You, too, can create a frightening presence with these gruesome folds.

you will need:
- Square of paper, plain on one side and colored on the other

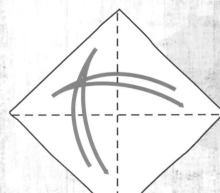

1 Fold and unfold the square in half from corner to corner, plain side up.

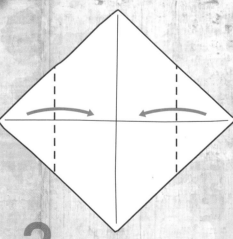

2 Valley fold the right- and left-hand corners in to the middle.

3 Valley fold the sides in to the middle.

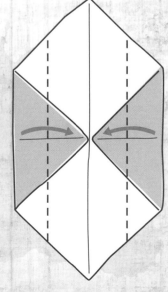

4

Turn the paper around 90° clockwise. Valley fold the top and bottom edges in to the middle.

5
Valley fold the left-hand corner over to a point ...

6
one-third of the way from the right.

7
Turn the paper over. Valley fold the right-hand corner to the left as shown, making the handle.

8

Narrow down the handle by valley folding its top and bottom edges in to the middle, making the adjoining points rise up. Flatten them down in to triangles.

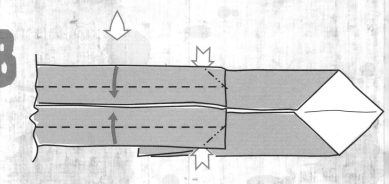

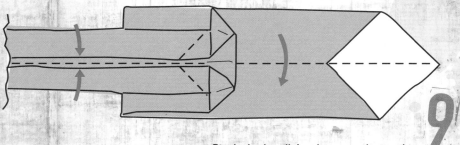

9

Pinch the handle's edges together, making it stand upright. Valley fold the underneath section of paper in half from top to bottom.

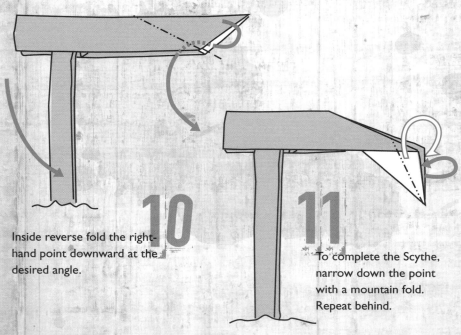

10

Inside reverse fold the right-hand point downward at the desired angle.

11

To complete the Scythe, narrow down the point with a mountain fold. Repeat behind.

Arrange the Hooded Grim Reaper and Scythe together as shown.

A scythe represents that the grim reaper has come to harvest lives

Slimy Hand

Here is a fun way to make a macabre slimy hand for that spooky night. It may have the power to unlock any door that it comes across and can render anyone motionless when it's presented to them!

you will need:
- Square of paper, plain on one side and colored on the other

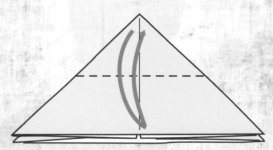

1 Begin by repeating steps 7 to 11 of the Evil Witch's Cat on page 28, with the square. Valley fold the top point down to meet the middle of the bottom edge. Press flat and unfold.

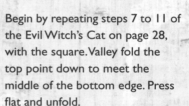

2 Sink the top point. To do this, unfold the paper ...

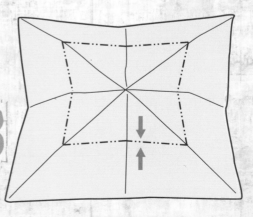

3 and flatten out the top point. Crease the four edges of the inner square in to mountain folds.

4 Push down on the middle of the square, at the same time pushing in the sides, so that they collapse toward the middle. Keep on pushing until the square fully collapses, thereby inverting the top point inside the waterbomb base.

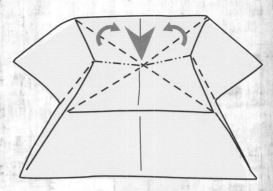

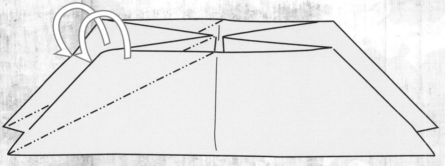

5 Narrow down the left-hand flaps with mountain folds as shown.

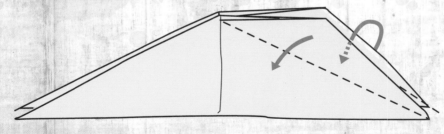

6 Narrow down the right-hand flaps with valley folds as shown.

7 Valley fold one right-hand flap over the left.

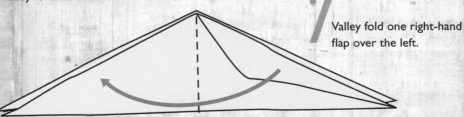

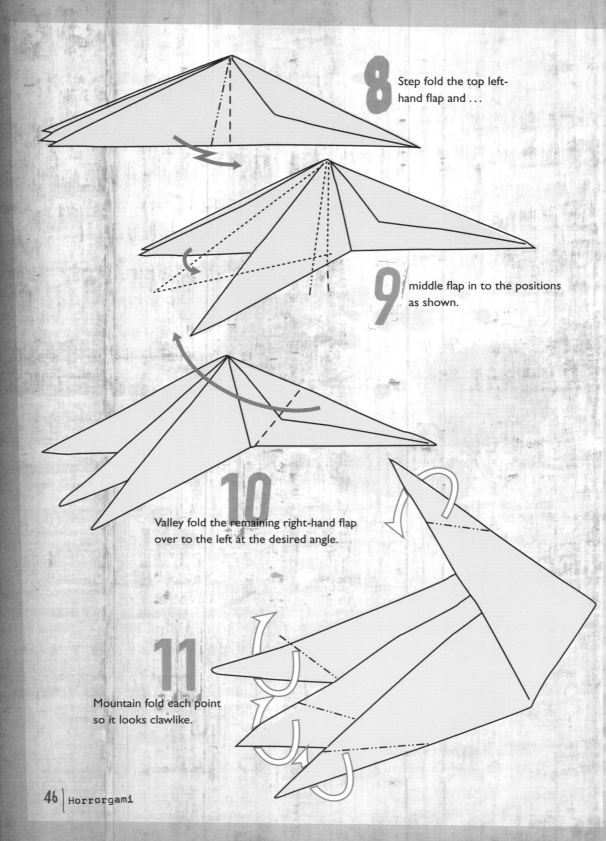

8 Step fold the top left-hand flap and . . .

9 middle flap in to the positions as shown.

10 Valley fold the remaining right-hand flap over to the left at the desired angle.

11 Mountain fold each point so it looks clawlike.

12 Turn the paper around 90° clockwise. To complete the Slimy Hand, mountain fold its bottom point behind a little.

Lady Fingers
was the love of
The Thing
in the popular TV series
The Addams Family

Fearsome Fangs

If you're looking for an awesome invitation card, or trying to play a trick, then make these amazing fangs. Who wouldn't want to look like an immortal vampire and greet everyone they meet with a big smile?

you will need:
● Square of paper, plain on one side and colored on the other

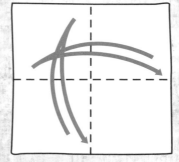

1 Fold and unfold the square in half from side to side and top to bottom, plain side up.

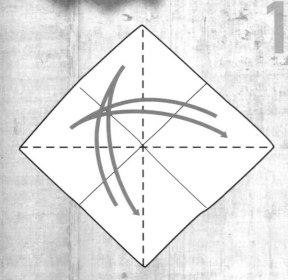

2 Turn the square around 90° clockwise. Fold and unfold it in half from corner to corner.

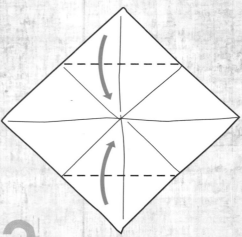

3 Valley fold the top and bottom corners in to the middle.

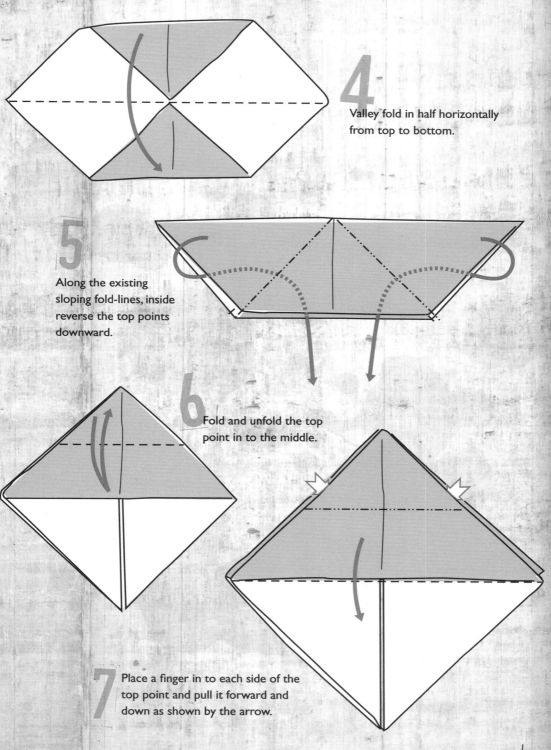

4 Valley fold in half horizontally from top to bottom.

5 Along the existing sloping fold-lines, inside reverse the top points downward.

6 Fold and unfold the top point in to the middle.

7 Place a finger in to each side of the top point and pull it forward and down as shown by the arrow.

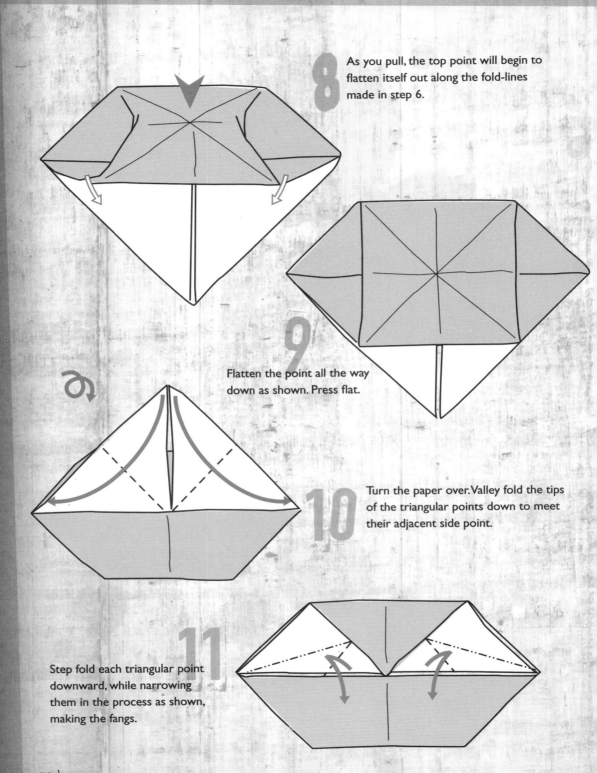

8 As you pull, the top point will begin to flatten itself out along the fold-lines made in step 6.

9 Flatten the point all the way down as shown. Press flat.

10 Turn the paper over. Valley fold the tips of the triangular points down to meet their adjacent side point.

11 Step fold each triangular point downward, while narrowing them in the process as shown, making the fangs.

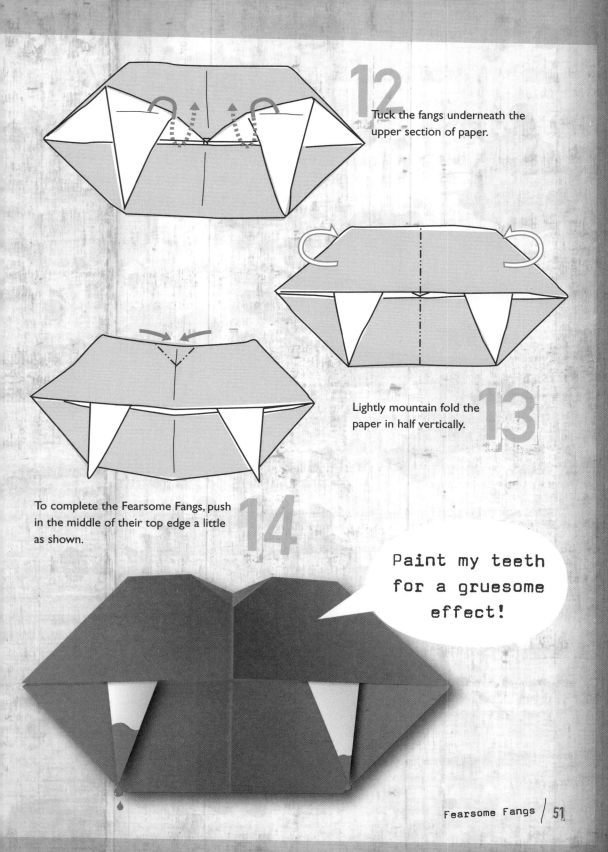

12

Tuck the fangs underneath the upper section of paper.

13

Lightly mountain fold the paper in half vertically.

14

To complete the Fearsome Fangs, push in the middle of their top edge a little as shown.

Paint my teeth for a gruesome effect!

Gruesome Raven

This carrion eater has a symbiotic relationship with man's old enemy, the wolf. It represents darkness, destructiveness, and evil. Many witches have been known to take on its form, so you have been warned!

you will need:
- Square of paper, plain on one side and colored on the other

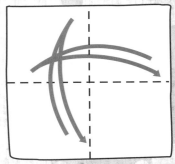

1 Fold and unfold the square in half from side to side and top to bottom, plain side up.

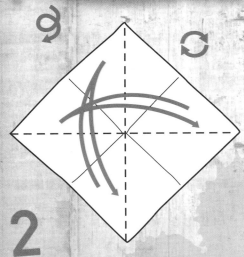

2 Turn the square over and around 90° clockwise. Fold and unfold it in half from corner to corner.

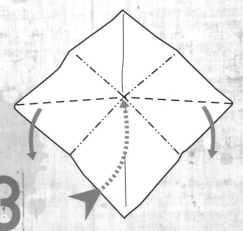

3 From below, push up on the square at its middle point so that the mountain folds in the paper will flex gently, becoming convex. Now, using the existing fold-lines, carefully collapse the paper down in to . . .

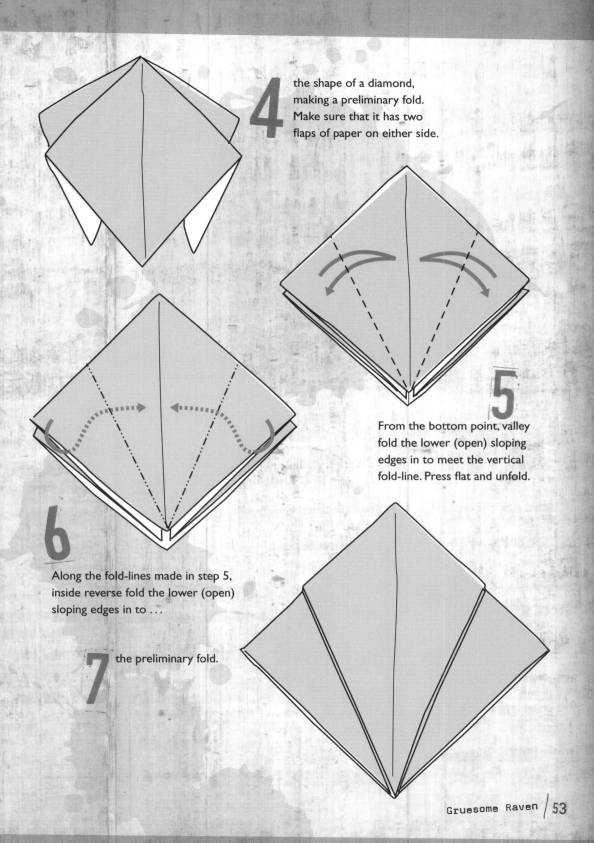

4 the shape of a diamond, making a preliminary fold. Make sure that it has two flaps of paper on either side.

5 From the bottom point, valley fold the lower (open) sloping edges in to meet the vertical fold-line. Press flat and unfold.

6 Along the fold-lines made in step 5, inside reverse fold the lower (open) sloping edges in to . . .

7 the preliminary fold.

8 Turn the paper over. Repeat steps 5 and 6, making . . .

9 a bird base. Valley fold the front flap up on a line between the two side points.

10 Valley fold the two lower points out to either side as shown, making . . .

11 the legs.

12 Turn the paper over. Mountain fold the middle point behind a little.

13 Step fold the top point as shown, making the beak.

14

Mountain fold in half
from left to right.

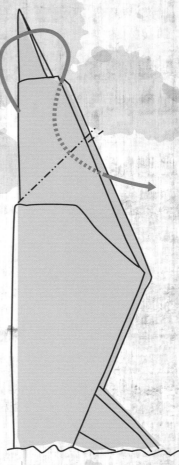

15

Inside reverse fold the
beak downward at the
desired angle.

16

Shape the legs by valley folding
their tips over a little.

17 The completed
Gruesome Raven.

Messenger of
death and
ill omens

Sinister Skull

You may decide to leave this ghastly and chilling model on display all the time, perhaps in a cupboard or behind a door someplace. It's sure to surprise anyone who isn't expecting it.

you will need:

- Two squares of paper, identical in size, plain on one side and colored on the other

- Glue stick

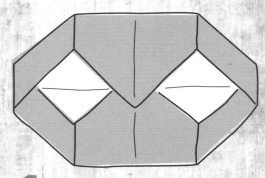

1 **Skull:** Begin by repeating steps 2 to 5 of the Jack-o'-Lantern on page 16, with one square.

2 **Teeth:** Turn the remaining square around so that one corner is toward you, plain side up. Fold and unfold it in half from corner to corner.

the skull
represents death
and mortality
throughout history

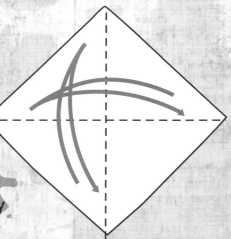

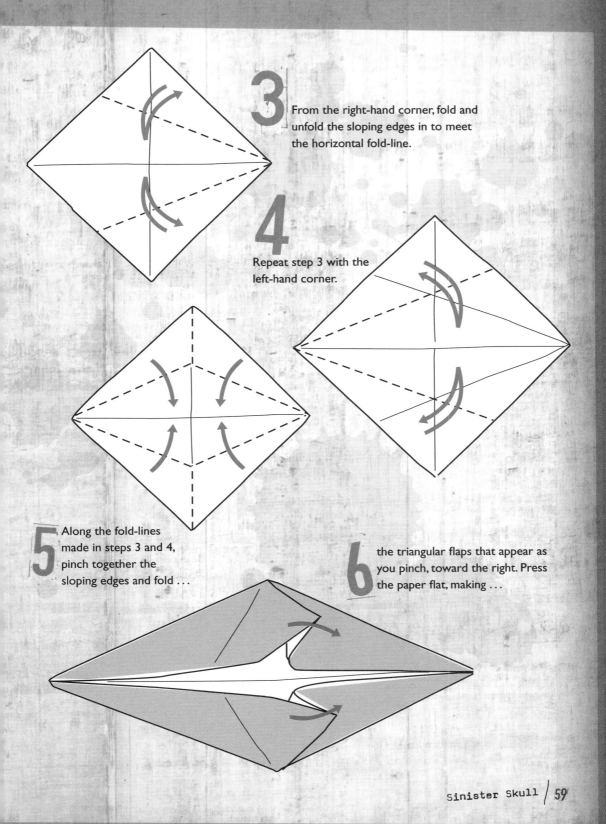

3 From the right-hand corner, fold and unfold the sloping edges in to meet the horizontal fold-line.

4 Repeat step 3 with the left-hand corner.

5 Along the fold-lines made in steps 3 and 4, pinch together the sloping edges and fold . . .

6 the triangular flaps that appear as you pinch, toward the right. Press the paper flat, making . . .

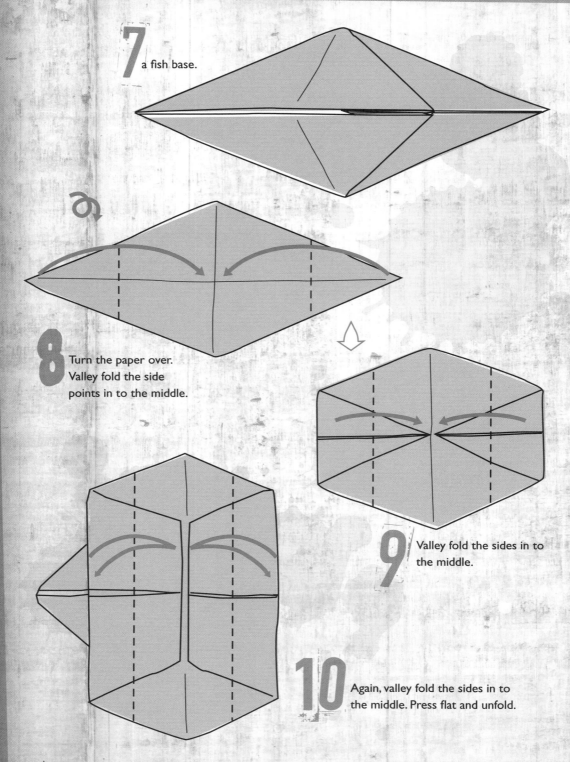

7 a fish base.

8 Turn the paper over. Valley fold the side points in to the middle.

9 Valley fold the sides in to the middle.

10 Again, valley fold the sides in to the middle. Press flat and unfold.

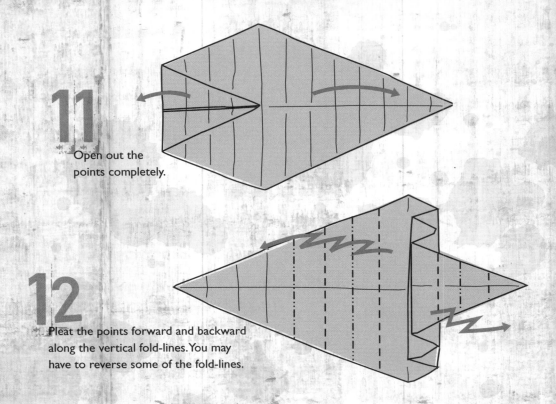

11 Open out the points completely.

12 Pleat the points forward and backward along the vertical fold-lines. You may have to reverse some of the fold-lines.

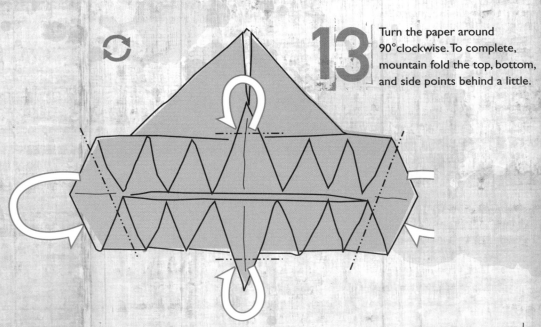

13 Turn the paper around 90° clockwise. To complete, mountain fold the top, bottom, and side points behind a little.

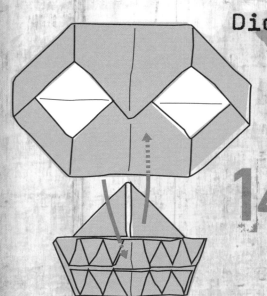

Did you know that
the human skull
is composed
of 22 bones?

14 To complete the Sinister Skull, slip the skull behind the teeth a little and glue both parts together.

They call me
Bones

Rattling Bones

Does your crypt or graveyard lack that sinister appearance so important to frightening away visitors? Has your attic or cellar lost its terrifying atmosphere of inescapable condemnation? Perhaps all you need are a few bones scattered about! And now you can fold as many as you wish.

you will need:
- Square of paper, white on both sides
- Scissors

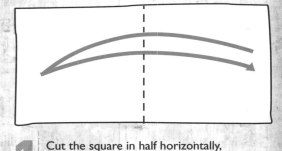

1 Cut the square in half horizontally, making two rectangles. Turn one rectangle sideways on. Valley fold it in half vertically, then unfold.

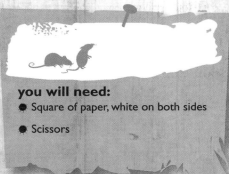

2 Valley fold in half horizontally from bottom to top.

The **longest** and **strongest** bone in the human body is the **femur bone** in the thigh

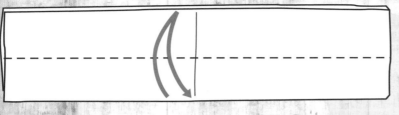

3 Valley fold in half horizontally from bottom to top, then unfold.

4 Valley fold the bottom edge up to meet the adjacent horizontal fold-line, making a pleat in the paper.

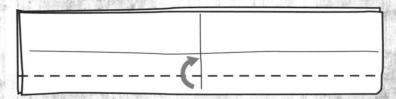

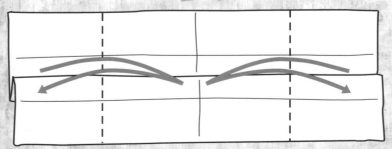

5 Open out the paper from the top, taking care not to unfold the pleat.

6 Fold and unfold the sides in to meet the vertical fold-line.

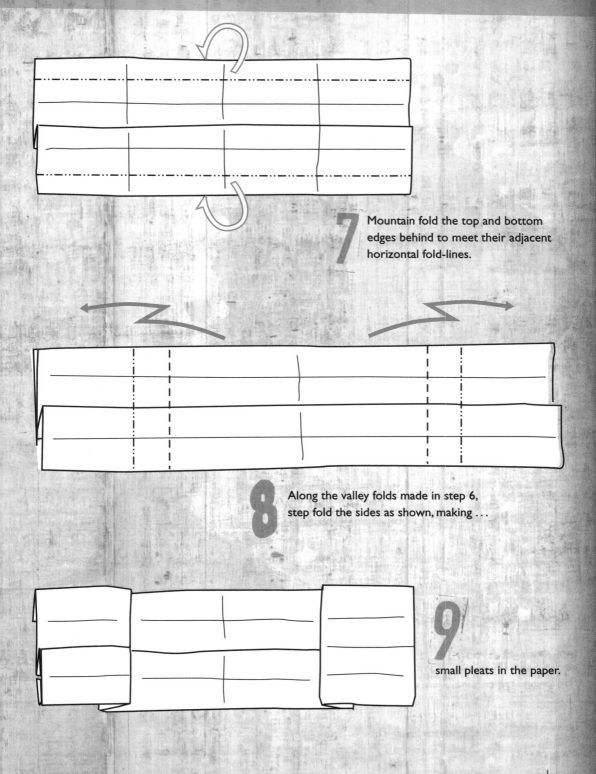

7 Mountain fold the top and bottom edges behind to meet their adjacent horizontal fold-lines.

8 Along the valley folds made in step 6, step fold the sides as shown, making . . .

9 small pleats in the paper.

10 Turn the paper over. Narrow down the paper's middle section by valley folding its top and bottom edges in to meet the horizontal fold-line, making their adjoining points rise up. Flatten them …

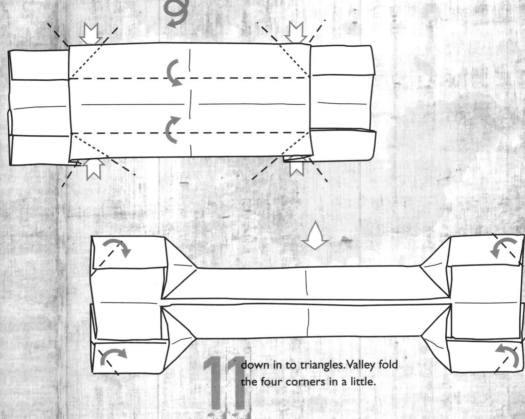

11 down in to triangles. Valley fold the four corners in a little.

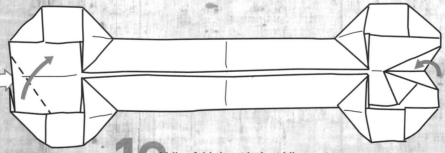

12 Valley fold the sides' middle sections over on a slant, while at the same time pressing them down in to "V-like" shapes as shown on the illustration's right-hand side.

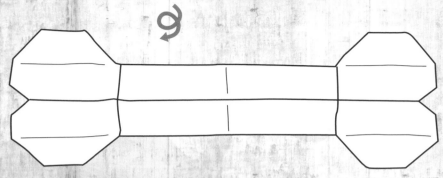

9

13 To complete the Rattling Bones, turn them over. Now make a further set of bones with the remaining rectangle of paper.

An adult human **skeleton** has over 200 **bones**

Howling Werewolf

A werewolf is a mythological or folkloric human often attributed with superhuman strength and the ability to shapeshift into a wolf or an anthropomorphic wolf-like creature, either purposely, by being bitten by another werewolf, or after being placed under a curse. Are you ready to be transformed in to one by the light of a full moon?

you will need:
- Square of paper, plain on one side and colored on the other

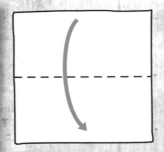

1 Valley fold the square in half horizontally from top to bottom, plain side up.

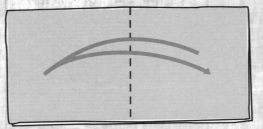

2 Valley fold in half vertically, then unfold.

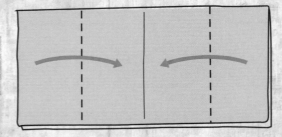

3 Valley fold the sides in to meet the vertical fold-line.

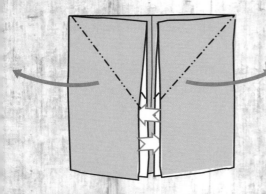

4 Open out the sides, pressing their tops down in to the shape of . . .

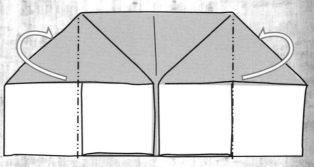

5 triangular roofs. Mountain fold the sides behind to meet the vertical fold-line.

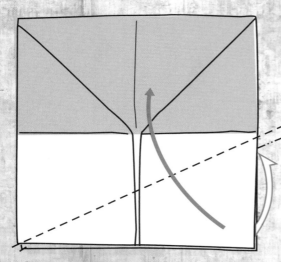

6 Valley fold the top layer of paper over on a line between the bottom left-hand corner and the middle of the right-hand side. Repeat behind.

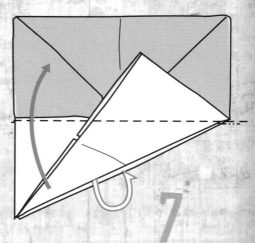

7 Valley fold the top layer of paper up to meet the top edge. Repeat behind.

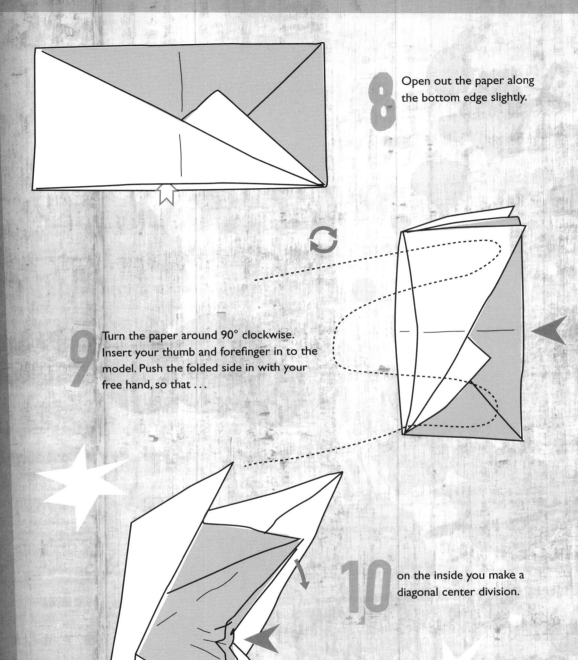

8 Open out the paper along the bottom edge slightly.

9 Turn the paper around 90° clockwise. Insert your thumb and forefinger in to the model. Push the folded side in with your free hand, so that . . .

10 on the inside you make a diagonal center division.

11

Here is the completed Howling Werewolf. To make the Werewolf appear to howl, rest him on the back of your free hand and move the forefinger that is inside him up and down, making the figure open and close its "mouth."

Why not draw on my features to add some **bite!**

"**We should never try the beast —the animal within us**"
Dr. George Waggner, *The Howling*

Maleficent Medusa

Medusa was the most famous of all the Greek gorgons and desecrated Athena's temple. Outraged, Athena turned Medusa's long, silky hair into living snakes and gave her destructive powers to turn anyone who looked directly at her eyes into stone.

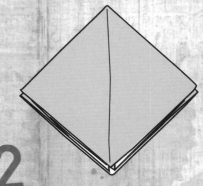

you will need:
- Two squares of paper, identical in size, plain on one side and colored on the other
- Scissors
- Glue stick

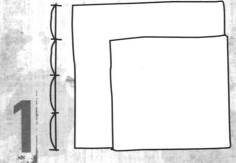

1 From one square, cut out a square for the face to the size shown.

2 **Face:** Begin by repeating steps 1 to 4 of the Gruesome Raven on page 52, with the face's square.

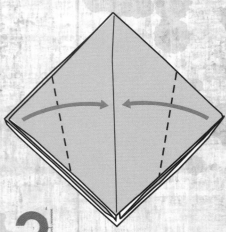

3 Valley fold the side points in on a slant, and ...

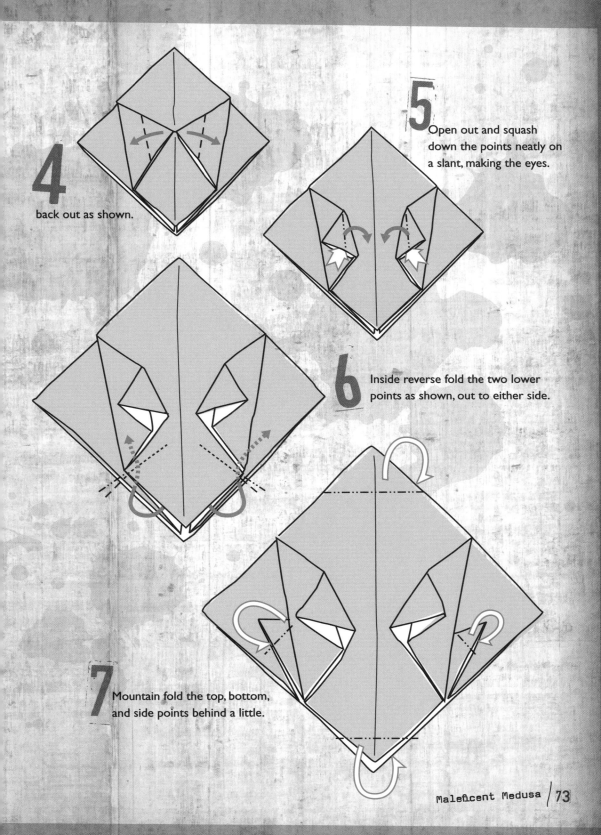

4

back out as shown.

5 Open out and squash down the points neatly on a slant, making the eyes.

6 Inside reverse fold the two lower points as shown, out to either side.

7 Mountain fold the top, bottom, and side points behind a little.

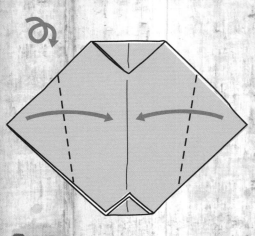

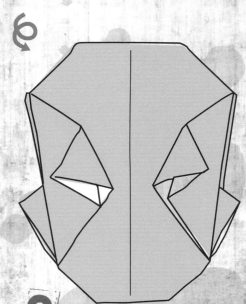

8 Turn the paper over. Aligning them up with the underneath sloping edges, valley fold the side points in on a slant.

9 To complete, turn the paper over.

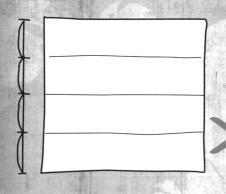

10 **Snakes:** Cut the remaining square in to quarters horizontally, making four rectangles.

11 Turn one rectangle sideways on, plain side up. Valley fold it in half horizontally, then unfold.

12 Valley fold the corners in to meet the horizontal fold-line.

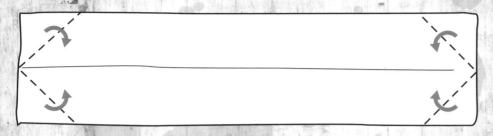

13 Turn the paper over. Valley fold the top and bottom edges in to meet the horizontal fold-line.

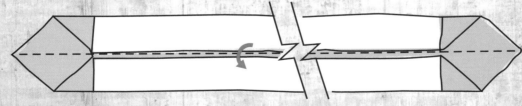

14 Valley fold in half from top to bottom.

15 Valley fold the corners over a little, making the eyes. Repeat behind.

16

Valley fold the left-hand point over to . . .

17

the right on a slant. Repeat steps 10 to 17 with the remaining three rectangles.

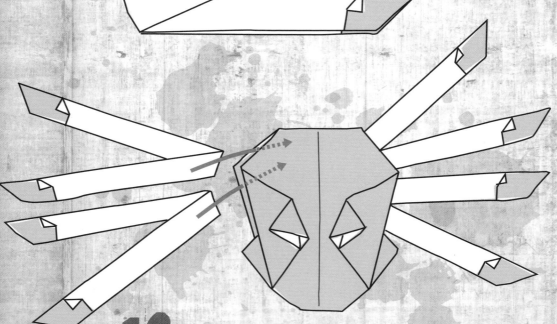

18

Glue the snakes, two either side, in-between the layers of Medusa's face as shown.

19 To complete Maleficent Medusa, fold the snakes to the desired angles.

Snakes, Rattle, and Roll!

Hooting Owl

Superstitions surrounding these nocturnal creatures have a long and ancient history. It's believed that they are the messengers for sorcerers and witches, who danced together on the graves of the dead. And that if you hear their spooky piercing cries, a ghost is approaching.

you will need:
- Square of paper, plain on one side and colored on the other
- Scissors

1 Begin by repeating steps 1 to 8 of the Gruesome Raven on page 52, with the square. From the top point, valley fold the sloping edges in to meet the vertical fold-line. Repeat behind.

2 Valley fold the top right-hand section of paper over to the opposite side.

3 Pull the lower point upward, at the same time making ...

4 the adjoining section of paper rise up. Press the paper . . .

5 down neatly as shown, making a wing. Repeat steps 2 to 5 with the top left-hand section of paper.

6 Valley fold the wings to point downward, covering the body a little.

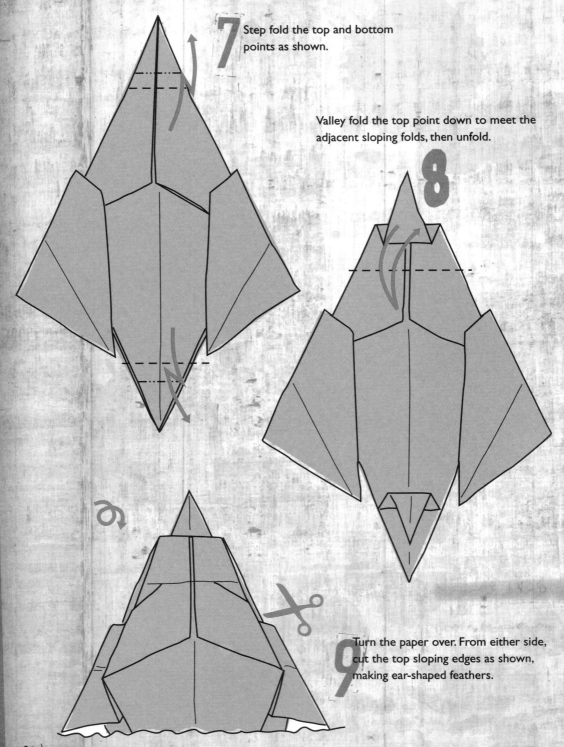

7 Step fold the top and bottom points as shown.

Valley fold the top point down to meet the adjacent sloping folds, then unfold.

8

9 Turn the paper over. From either side, cut the top sloping edges as shown, making ear-shaped feathers.

10 Turn the paper over. Along the fold-line made in step 8, valley fold the point down, making the ears protrude.

9

Hoot!
Hoot!

Owls are messengers
for
witches
and
sorcerers

Phantom of the Opera

He's a musical genius and magician who has a skull-like face and lives in the catacombs beneath Paris's Opera Populaire, known only as the Phantom of the Opera. As the ghost, he makes his living by stealing and demanding from the managers his share of the profit the opera house makes.

you will need:

● Two squares of paper, identical in size, plain on one side and colored on the other

● Scissors

● Glue stick

1 From one square, cut out a square for the face to the size shown.

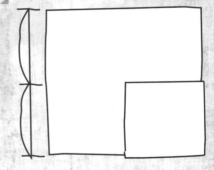

2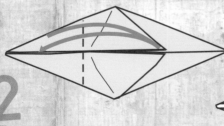

Face: Begin by repeating steps 2 to 7 of the Sinister Skull on page 58, with the face's square. Valley fold the left-hand point over to meet the tips of the triangular flaps, then unfold.

3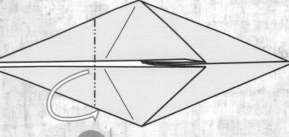

Along the vertical fold-line made in step 2, mountain fold the left-hand point behind.

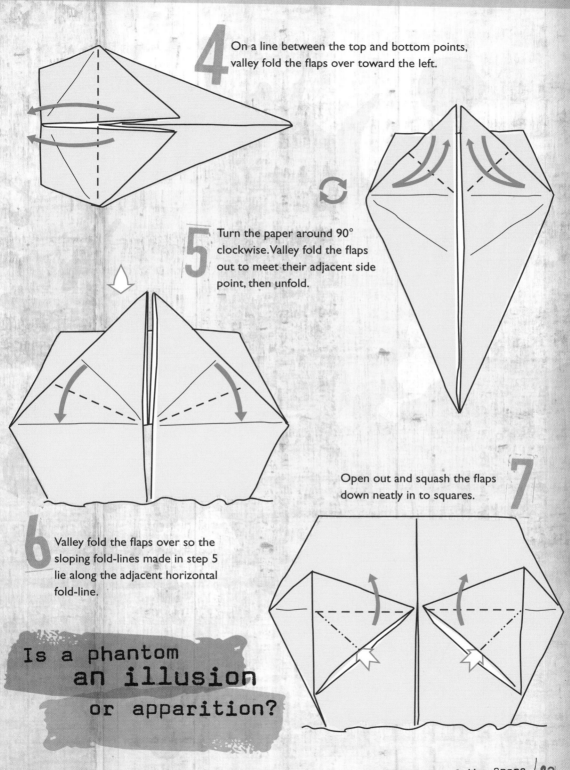

4 On a line between the top and bottom points, valley fold the flaps over toward the left.

5 Turn the paper around 90° clockwise. Valley fold the flaps out to meet their adjacent side point, then unfold.

6 Valley fold the flaps over so the sloping fold-lines made in step 5 lie along the adjacent horizontal fold-line.

7 Open out and squash the flaps down neatly in to squares.

Is a phantom an illusion or apparition?

8 Valley fold the top flap of the squashed points out, making the eyes.

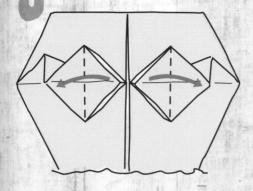

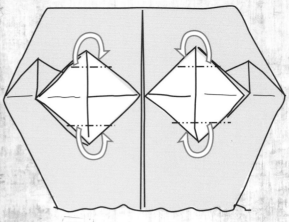

9 Mountain fold the eyes' upper and lower points behind a little.

10 Valley fold the bottom point up to meet the middle of the top edge.

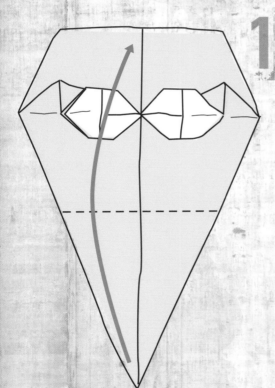

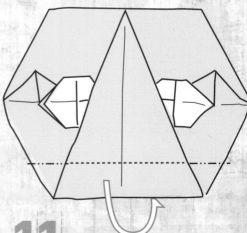

11 Mountain fold the bottom edge behind a little, at the same time letting the point flip down.

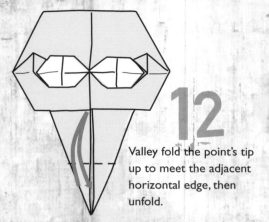

12

Valley fold the point's tip up to meet the adjacent horizontal edge, then unfold.

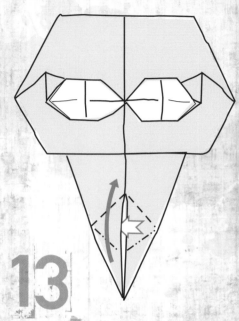

13

Open out the point, making the fold-lines as shown, at the same time pushing the point's tip . . .

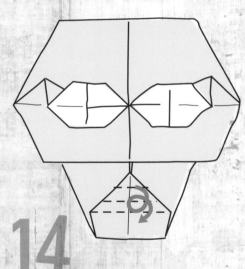

14

back toward the horizontal edge along the fold-line made in step 12. Valley fold the point's tip over and over itself, making the mouth.

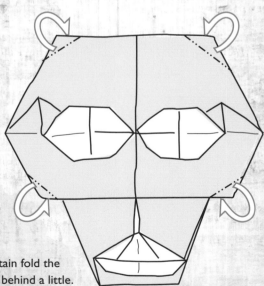

15

To complete, mountain fold the top and side points behind a little.

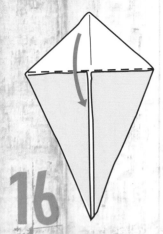

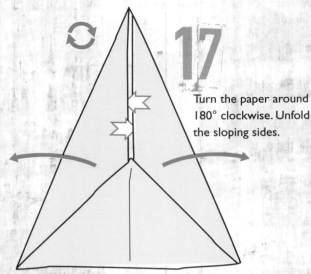

16

Cape: Begin by repeating steps 1 to 3 of the Friendly Ghost on page 10, with the remaining square, plain side up. Valley fold the top point down as shown.

17

Turn the paper around 180° clockwise. Unfold the sloping sides.

18

Valley fold the top point down to meet the triangle's tip and then ...

19

valley fold it back up a little.

20

Along the existing fold-lines, valley fold the sloping sides over.

21 To complete the Phantom of the Opera, glue the face onto the cape at the desired angle.

"We recognize the touch of the Opera ghost"
Gaston Leroux,
Phantom of the Opera

Fa la la, la la!

Ghastly Ghoul

Ghouls are folkloric monsters who are supposed to rob graves and prey on human corpses often believed to be the undead. They have coarse gray hair and long sharp fingernails. Just be careful when walking around a graveyard at night, as you may just bump into one!

you will need:

● Square of paper, plain on one side and colored on the other

● Scissors

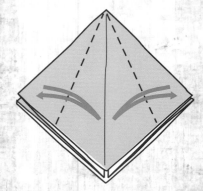

1 Begin by repeating steps 1 to 4 of the Gruesome Raven on page 52, with the square. From the top point, valley fold the upper (folded) sloping edges in to meet the vertical fold-line. Press flat and unfold.

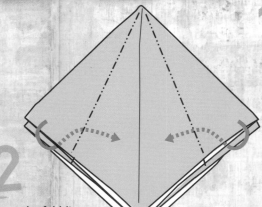

2 Along the fold-lines made in step 2, inside reverse fold the upper (folded) sloping edges in to the preliminary fold.

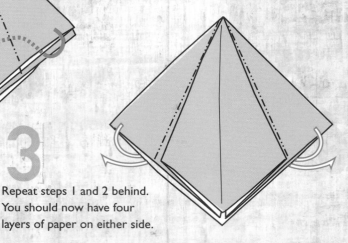

3 Repeat steps 1 and 2 behind. You should now have four layers of paper on either side.

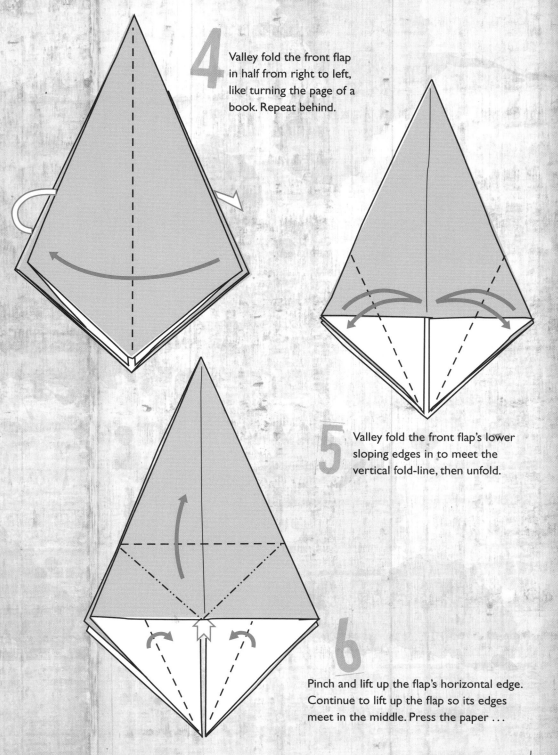

4 Valley fold the front flap in half from right to left, like turning the page of a book. Repeat behind.

5 Valley fold the front flap's lower sloping edges in to meet the vertical fold-line, then unfold.

6 Pinch and lift up the flap's horizontal edge. Continue to lift up the flap so its edges meet in the middle. Press the paper . . .

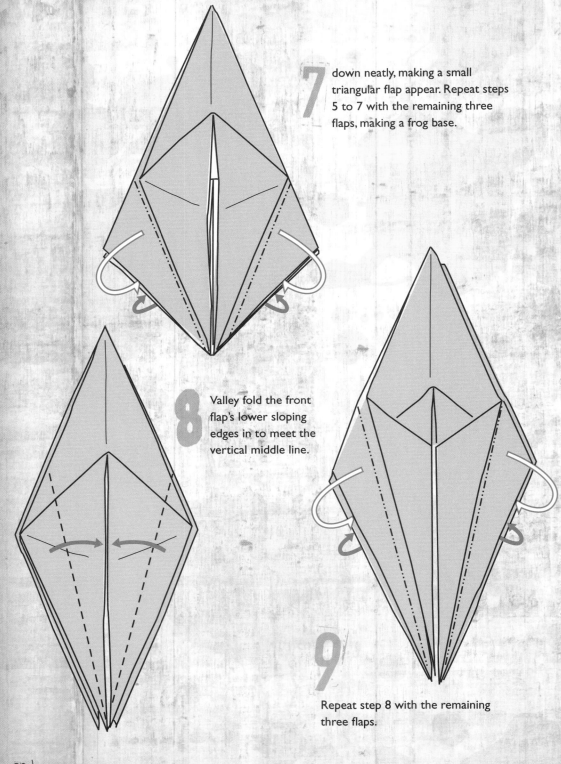

7 down neatly, making a small triangular flap appear. Repeat steps 5 to 7 with the remaining three flaps, making a frog base.

8 Valley fold the front flap's lower sloping edges in to meet the vertical middle line.

9 Repeat step 8 with the remaining three flaps.

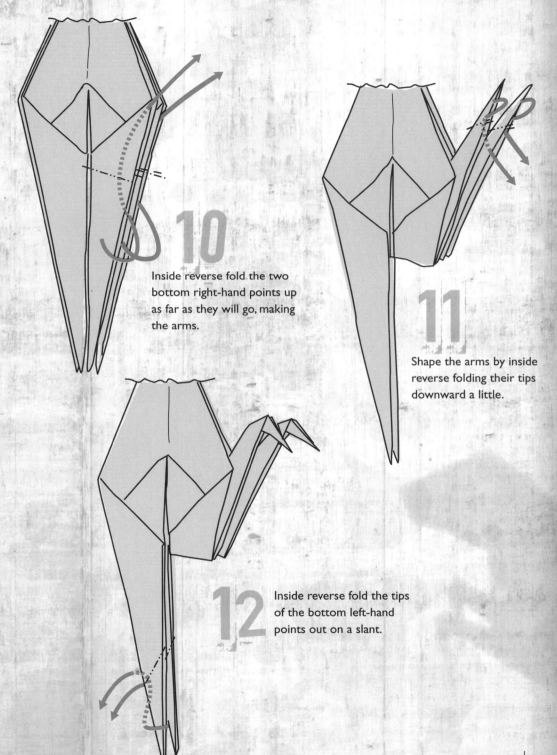

10 Inside reverse fold the two bottom right-hand points up as far as they will go, making the arms.

11 Shape the arms by inside reverse folding their tips downward a little.

12 Inside reverse fold the tips of the bottom left-hand points out on a slant.

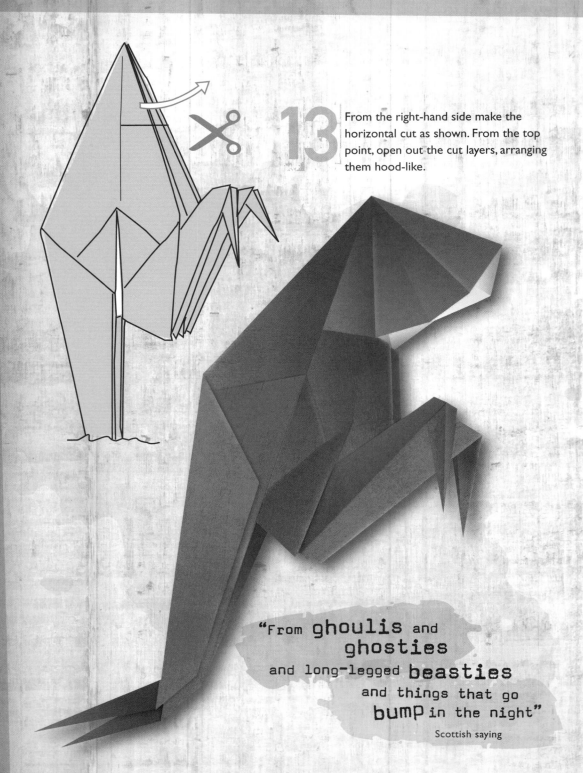

13 From the right-hand side make the horizontal cut as shown. From the top point, open out the cut layers, arranging them hood-like.

"From ghoulis and ghosties and long-legged beasties and things that go bump in the night"

Scottish saying

Daunting Demon's Head

The demon is a supernatural being from various religions and folklores that is described as something that is not human and, in ordinary (almost universal) usage, malevolent and can take on many forms.

you will need:
- Square of paper, plain on one side and colored on the other

1 Begin by repeating steps 1 to 8 of the Gruesome Raven on page 52, with the square. Valley fold the front flap up on a line between the two side points. Repeat behind.

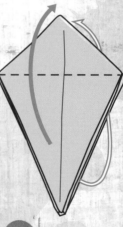

2 Valley fold the front flap in half from left to right, like turning the page of a book. Repeat behind.

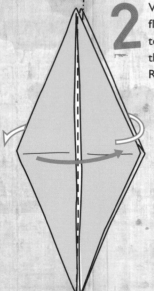

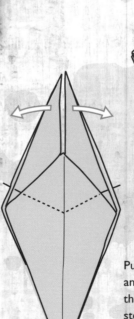

3 Pull the top points apart and press them flat in to the position as shown in step 4, making the horns.

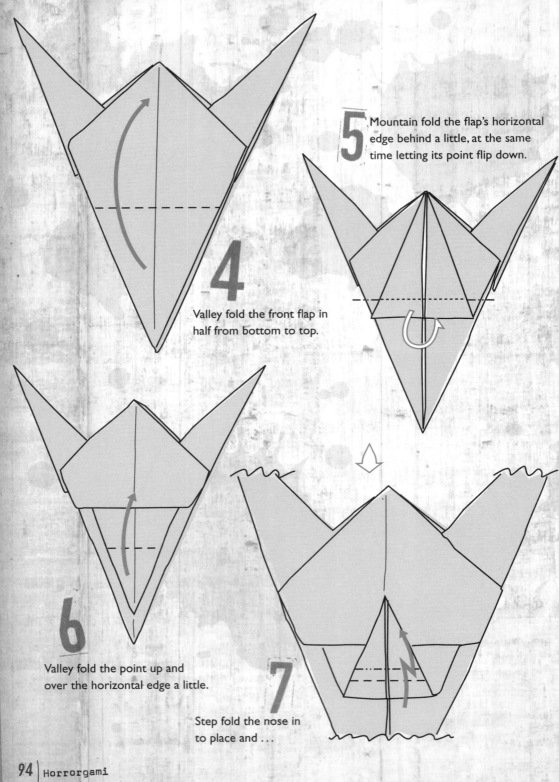

5 Mountain fold the flap's horizontal edge behind a little, at the same time letting its point flip down.

4 Valley fold the front flap in half from bottom to top.

6 Valley fold the point up and over the horizontal edge a little.

7 Step fold the nose in to place and . . .

8 tuck its tip underneath the horizontal edge. Valley fold either side of the edge over, making the eyes.

9 With a valley fold, tuck the bottom point underneath the nose.

10 Valley fold the top point down on a line between the horns.

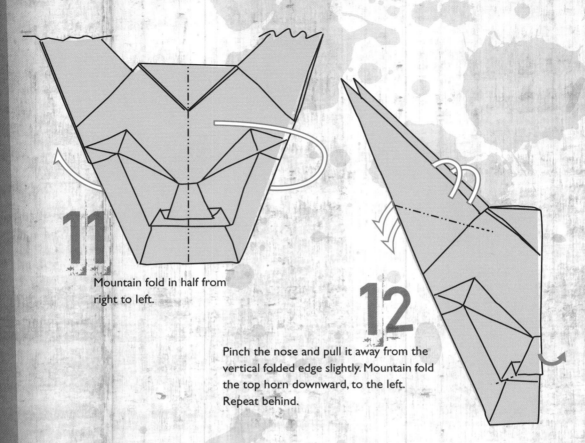

11

Mountain fold in half from right to left.

12

Pinch the nose and pull it away from the vertical folded edge slightly. Mountain fold the top horn downward, to the left. Repeat behind.

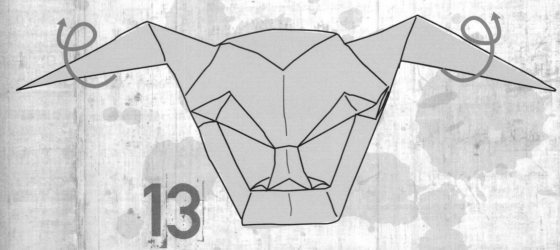

13

Open out the paper, but do not press it flat. Give the horns a gentle twist.

14

To complete the Daunting Demon's Head, mountain fold the side points behind a little.

Have **Evil** thoughts and make my day!

The ancient Greek word for "demon" means divine power

Frankenstein's Monster

Baron Victor Von Frankenstein wanted to create a being more beautiful then any human, but what he achieved was a monster. The monster was extremely gruesome in appearance. Its skin was yellow, muscles bulged out, and had a badly scarred (with stitches), shriveled face.

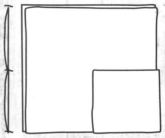

you will need:
- Three squares of paper, identical in size, plain on one side and colored on the other
- Scissors
- Glue stick

1 From one square, cut out a square for the head to the size shown.

2 **Head:** Begin by repeating steps 2 to 4 of Maleficent Medusa on page 72, with the head's square. Open out and squash down the points neatly on a slant, making droopily-like eyes.

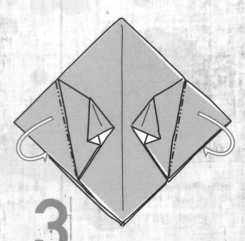

3 Aligning them up with the upper sloping edges, mountain fold the side points behind on a slant.

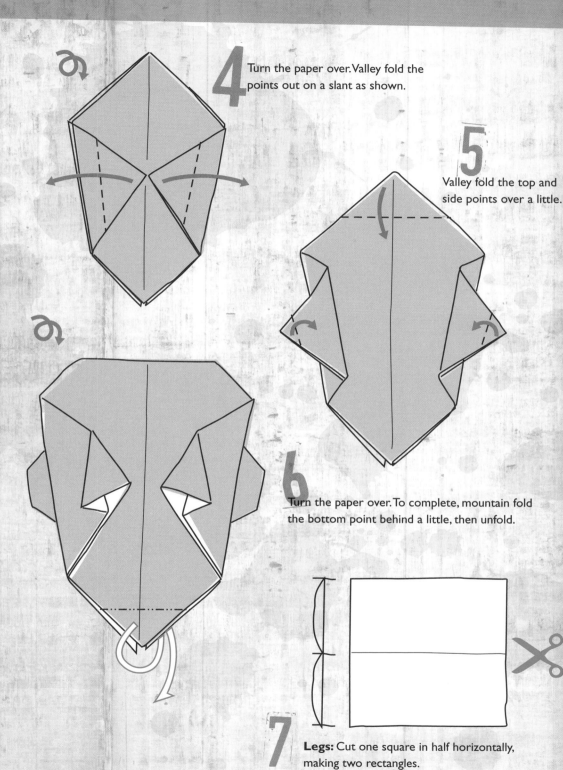

4 Turn the paper over. Valley fold the points out on a slant as shown.

5 Valley fold the top and side points over a little.

6 Turn the paper over. To complete, mountain fold the bottom point behind a little, then unfold.

7 Legs: Cut one square in half horizontally, making two rectangles.

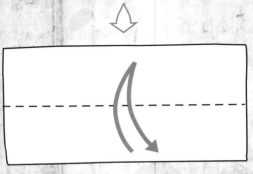

8

Turn one rectangle sideways on, plain side up. Valley fold it in half horizontally from bottom to top, then unfold.

9

Valley fold the left-hand corners in to meet the horizontal fold-line.

10

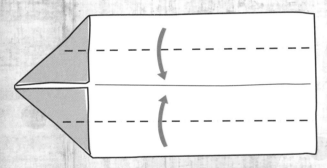

Valley fold the top and bottom edges in to meet the horizontal fold-line.

11

Step fold the left-hand point as shown, making a pleat.

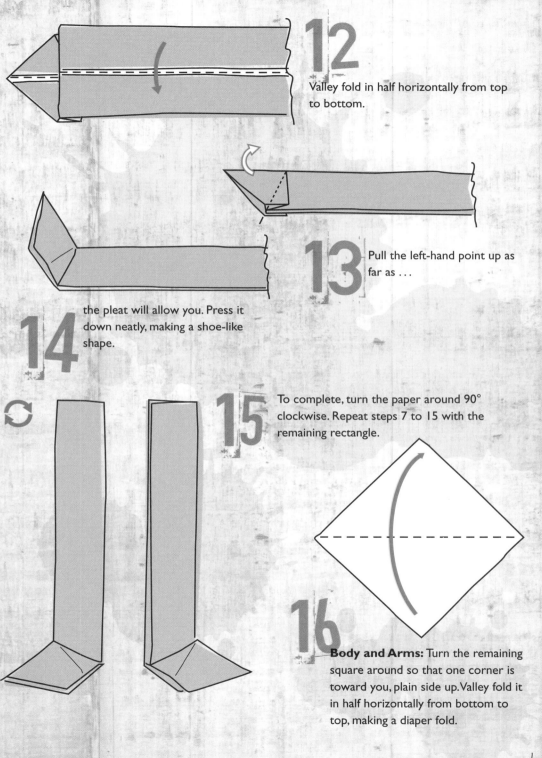

12
Valley fold in half horizontally from top to bottom.

13
Pull the left-hand point up as far as . . .

14
the pleat will allow you. Press it down neatly, making a shoe-like shape.

15
To complete, turn the paper around 90° clockwise. Repeat steps 7 to 15 with the remaining rectangle.

16
Body and Arms: Turn the remaining square around so that one corner is toward you, plain side up. Valley fold it in half horizontally from bottom to top, making a diaper fold.

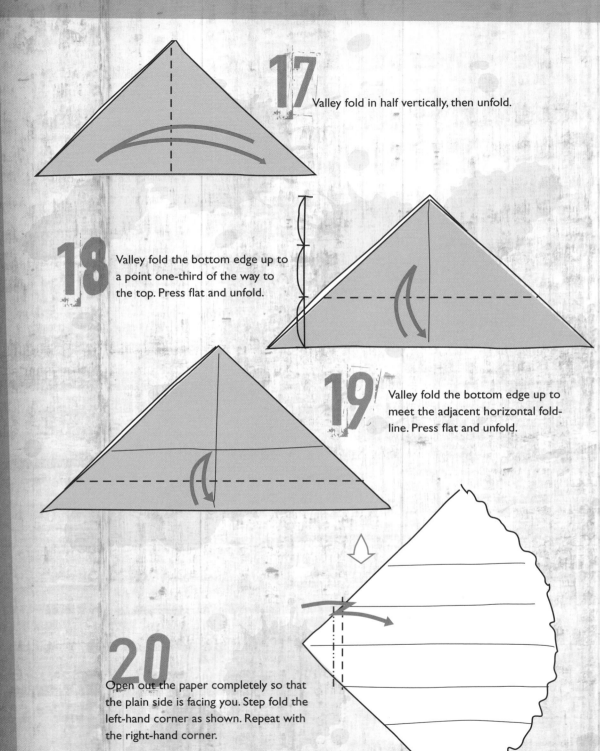

17 Valley fold in half vertically, then unfold.

18 Valley fold the bottom edge up to a point one-third of the way to the top. Press flat and unfold.

19 Valley fold the bottom edge up to meet the adjacent horizontal fold-line. Press flat and unfold.

20 Open out the paper completely so that the plain side is facing you. Step fold the left-hand corner as shown. Repeat with the right-hand corner.

21 Valley fold the left-hand corner over a little. Repeat with the right-hand corner.

Valley fold in half horizontally from bottom to top.

22

23 Along the fold-line made in step 18, mountain fold the top points behind.

24 Valley fold the horizontal edge up to meet the top edge, making the arms.

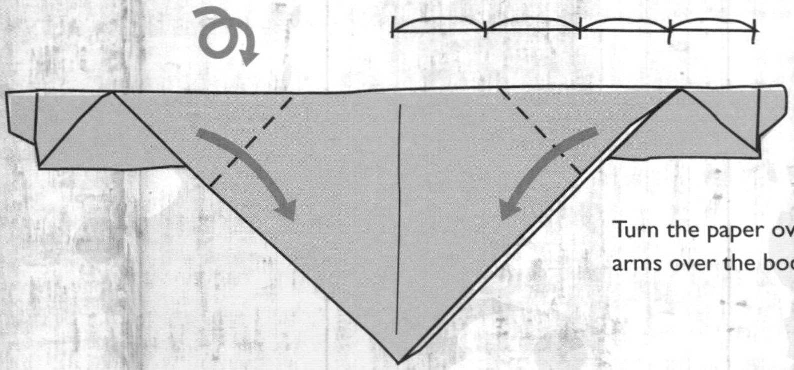

25

Turn the paper over. Valley fold the arms over the body as far as shown.

26

This should be your result.

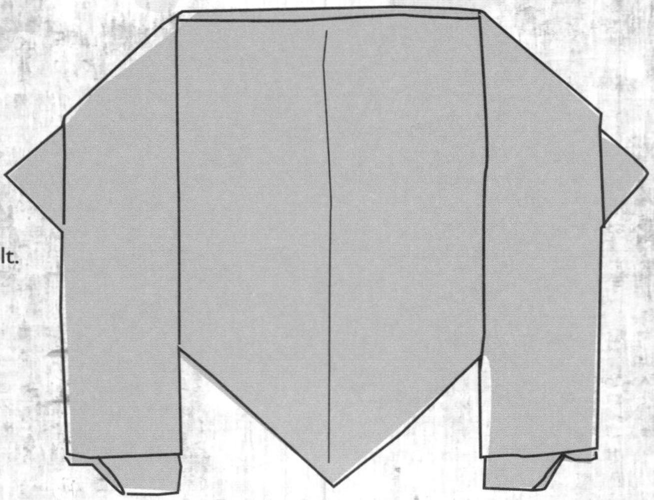

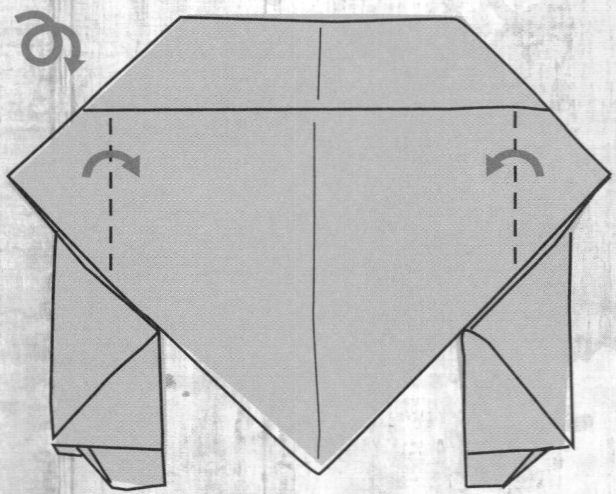

27

To complete, turn the paper over. Valley fold the side points over the body a little.

28

To complete Frankenstein's Monster, turn the body and arms over. Insert the head's bottom points between the body's top layers and the legs between its bottom layers as shown. Glue all parts together.

Fold me up and bring me to **life!**

Legends **Boris Karloff,** Lon Chaney, Jr., and **Bela Lugosi** have all played the role of **Frankenstein's monster**

The Mummy

The Ancient Egyptians believed that the body was the receptacle for the Ka, which was necessary for the afterlife. Skilled embalmers prepared the body by removing the internal organs, eliminating excess moisture with salts, and then wrapping the body with linens soaked in resin.

you will need:
- A rectangle of paper, about 11.7 x 8.3in, plain on one side and colored on the other

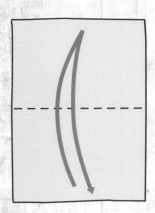

1

Place the rectangle lengthwise on, colored side up. Valley fold it in half horizontally from bottom to top, then unfold.

2

Valley fold the top and bottom edges in to meet the horizontal fold-line. Press flat and unfold.

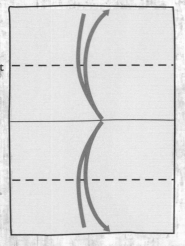

3

Carefully make the valley folds as shown.

4 Turn the paper over. Along the fold-lines made in steps 1 to 3, step fold the paper as shown, making . . .

5 seven pleats. Valley fold the right-hand side over toward the left. Valley fold the left-hand side over so that it lies on top.

6 Valley fold the lower pleats' sides in toward the middle, making their adjoining layers raise up. Flatten them . . .

7 down crookedly. Step fold the upper pleats as shown.

8 Valley fold the upper pleats' sides in toward the middle, making their adjoining layers rise up. Flatten them . . .

9 down in to triangles. Valley fold the top points over a little.

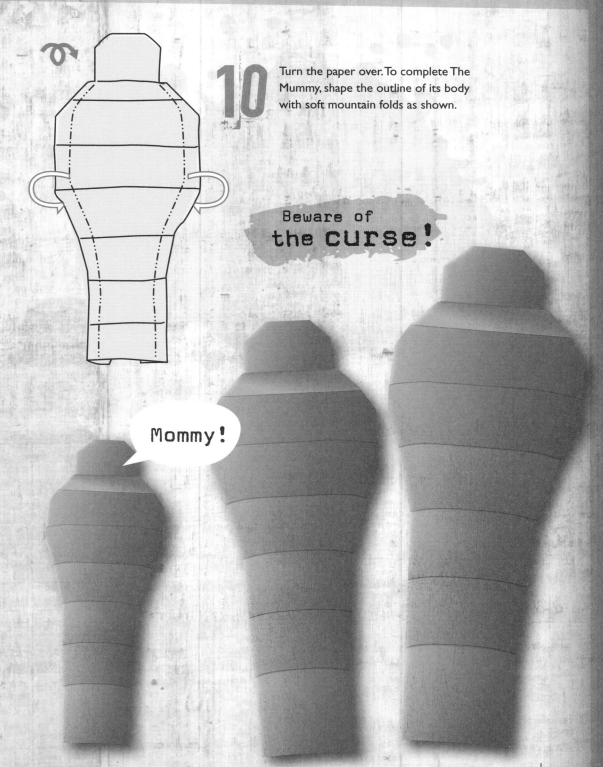

10 Turn the paper over. To complete The Mummy, shape the outline of its body with soft mountain folds as shown.

Beware of the **CURSE**!

Mommy!

Creepy Coffin

There's something really unsettling about old-fashioned toe-pincher coffins. Up until the 19th century carpenters built them to order for the newly deceased. Creepy coffin props are an essential piece of any macabre party decor, house haunting, or to simply sit in your front yard.

you will need:
- Two squares of paper, identical in size, plain on one side and colored on the other

1 **Lid:** Begin by repeating steps 1 to 3 of the Reaper's Scythe on page 40, with one square. Turn the paper sideways on. Valley fold the left-hand corner over to meet the right-hand sloping edges as shown. Press flat and unfold.

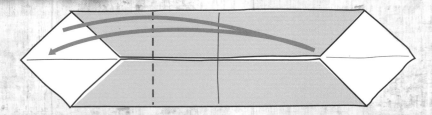

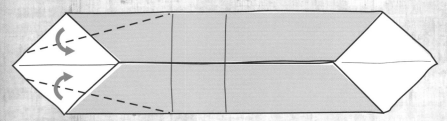

2 Using the fold-line made in step 1 as a location point, valley fold the left-hand top and bottom points in to meet the horizontal fold-line, on a slant.

3

Repeat step 2 with
the right-hand top
and bottom points.

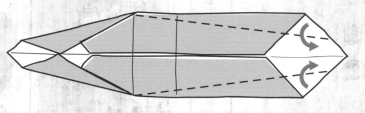

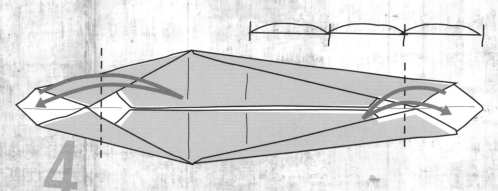

4

Valley fold the left-hand corner over to meet the fold-
line made in step 1, then unfold. Valley fold the right-
hand corner over to a point one-third of the way to
the middle. Press flat and unfold.

5

Unfold the right- and left-
hand sloping edges.

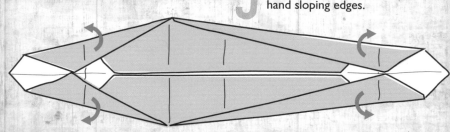

6

Along the fold-lines
made in step 4, fold
the right- and left-hand
corners back over.

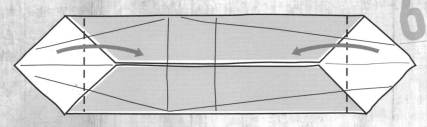

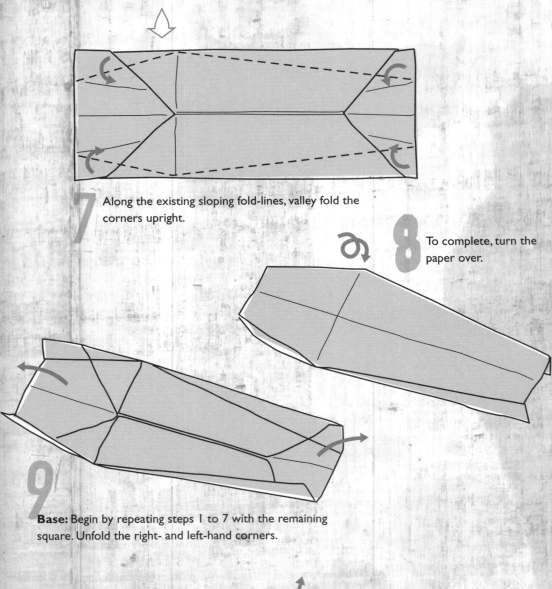

7 Along the existing sloping fold-lines, valley fold the corners upright.

8 To complete, turn the paper over.

9 **Base:** Begin by repeating steps 1 to 7 with the remaining square. Unfold the right- and left-hand corners.

10 Unfold the horizontal middle edges.

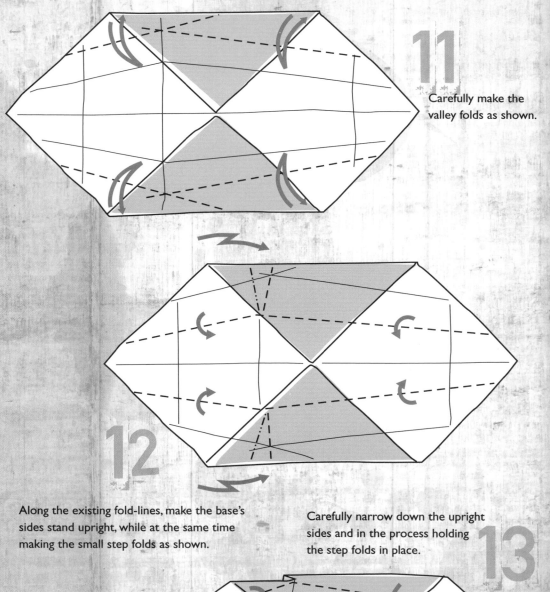

11

Carefully make the
valley folds as shown.

12

Along the existing fold-lines, make the base's
sides stand upright, while at the same time
making the small step folds as shown.

Carefully narrow down the upright
sides and in the process holding
the step folds in place.

13

14

Form the left-hand side of the base as shown.

15

Mountain fold the corner in to the base so locking all the folds together.

16

To complete, repeat steps 14 and 15 at the opposite end of the paper, making the base's right-hand side.

17

To complete the Creepy Coffin, place the lid on top of the base.

Toe-pincher coffins are also called **vampire coffins**

Sleep!

Zombie

You can only move around at night and must return to your grave before sunrise. A shoulder is dislocated trying to escape a Zombie's clammy grasp and an arm hangs limply at your side. Take care, as no matter who you are, you're at risk and will probably become one of the undead eventually.

you will need:

- Four squares of paper, identical in size, plain on one side and colored on the other

- Scissors

- Glue stick

1 From one square, cut out a square for the head to the size shown.

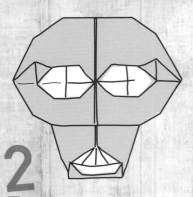

2 **Head:** Repeat steps 1 to 14 of the Phantom of the Opera on page 82, with the head's square.

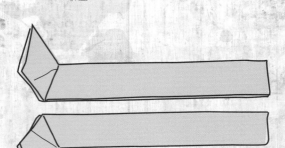

3 **Legs:** Repeat steps 7 to 15 of Frankenstein's Monster on page 99, with another square.

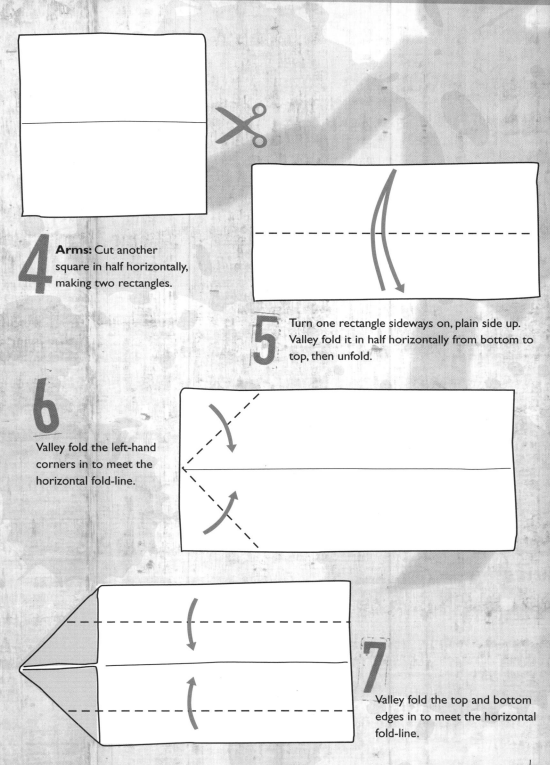

4 **Arms:** Cut another square in half horizontally, making two rectangles.

5 Turn one rectangle sideways on, plain side up. Valley fold it in half horizontally from bottom to top, then unfold.

6 Valley fold the left-hand corners in to meet the horizontal fold-line.

7 Valley fold the top and bottom edges in to meet the horizontal fold-line.

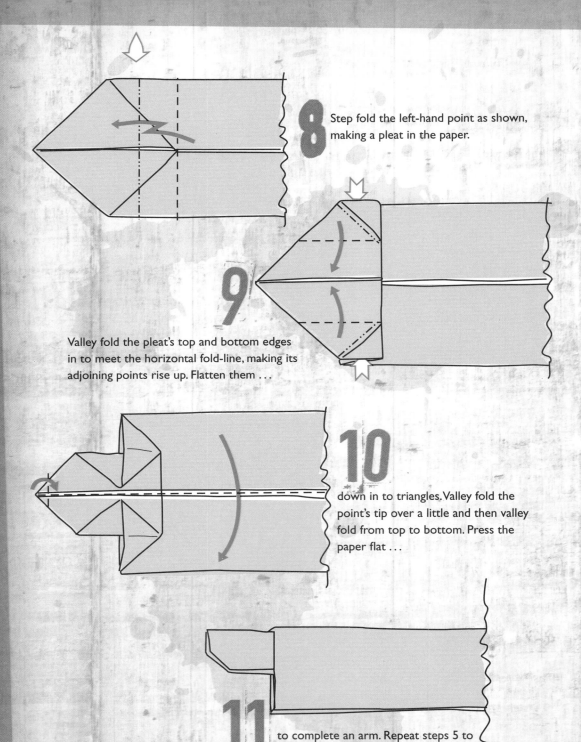

8 Step fold the left-hand point as shown, making a pleat in the paper.

9 Valley fold the pleat's top and bottom edges in to meet the horizontal fold-line, making its adjoining points rise up. Flatten them . . .

10 down in to triangles. Valley fold the point's tip over a little and then valley fold from top to bottom. Press the paper flat . . .

11 to complete an arm. Repeat steps 5 to 11 with the remaining rectangle.

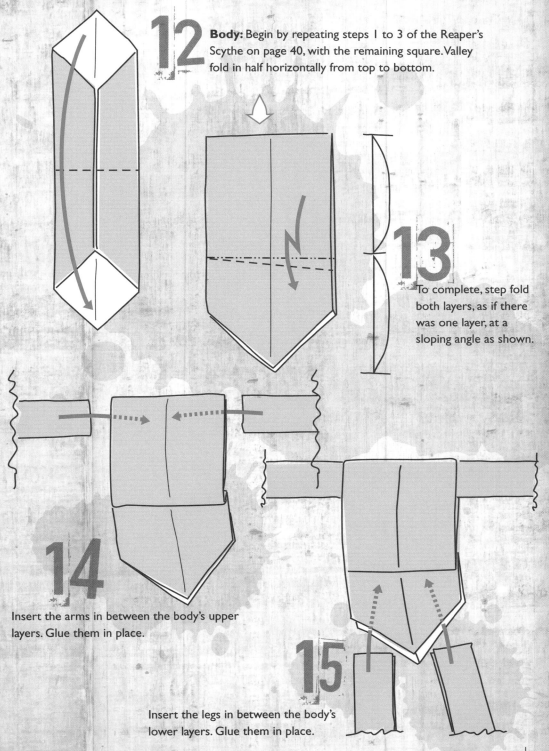

12 **Body:** Begin by repeating steps 1 to 3 of the Reaper's Scythe on page 40, with the remaining square. Valley fold in half horizontally from top to bottom.

13 To complete, step fold both layers, as if there was one layer, at a sloping angle as shown.

14 Insert the arms in between the body's upper layers. Glue them in place.

15 Insert the legs in between the body's lower layers. Glue them in place.

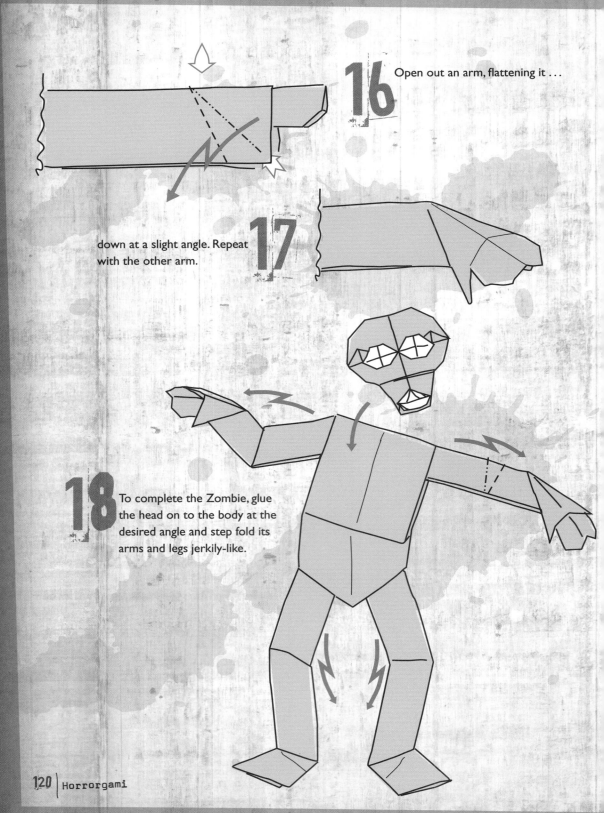

16 Open out an arm, flattening it . . .

17 down at a slight angle. Repeat with the other arm.

18 To complete the Zombie, glue the head on to the body at the desired angle and step fold its arms and legs jerkily-like.

Stupefying Spider

This evil spider is unafraid of any predator—including man—and no one is safe from its paralyzing sting, especially among those who suffer from arachnophobia; an acute fear of spiders. Beware of this creature's poison and the slow death it causes, the venom can often be seen as a curse.

you will need:
● Square of paper, plain on one side and colored on the other

● Scissors

1 Begin by repeating steps 1 to 9 of the Ghastly Ghoul on page 88, with the square. Unfold the front flap's lower sloping edges.

2 Valley fold the small triangular flap downward.

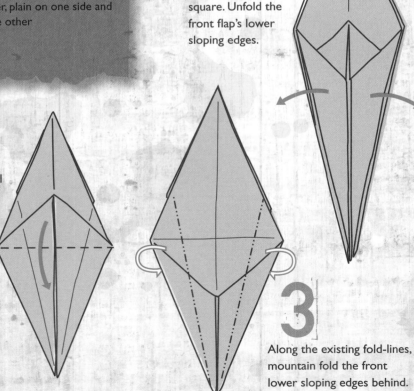

3 Along the existing fold-lines, mountain fold the front lower sloping edges behind.

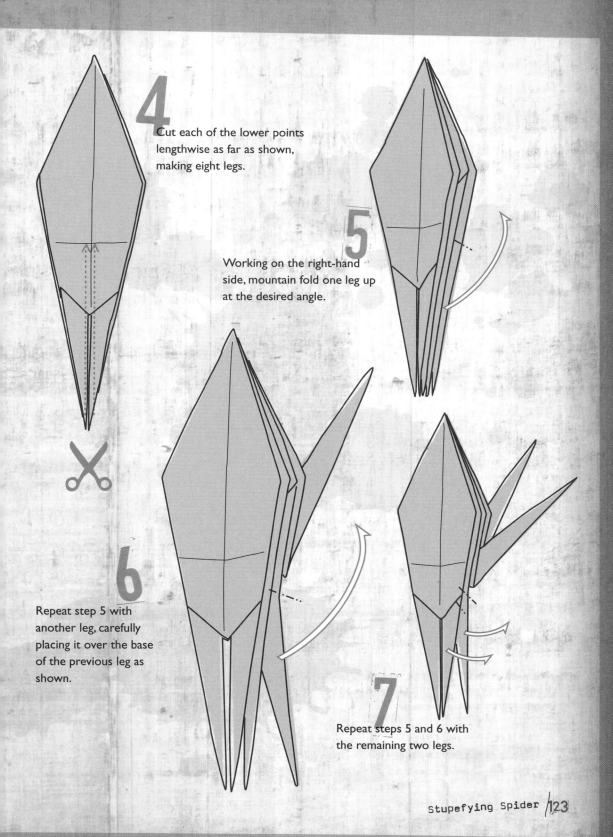

4 Cut each of the lower points lengthwise as far as shown, making eight legs.

5 Working on the right-hand side, mountain fold one leg up at the desired angle.

6 Repeat step 5 with another leg, carefully placing it over the base of the previous leg as shown.

7 Repeat steps 5 and 6 with the remaining two legs.

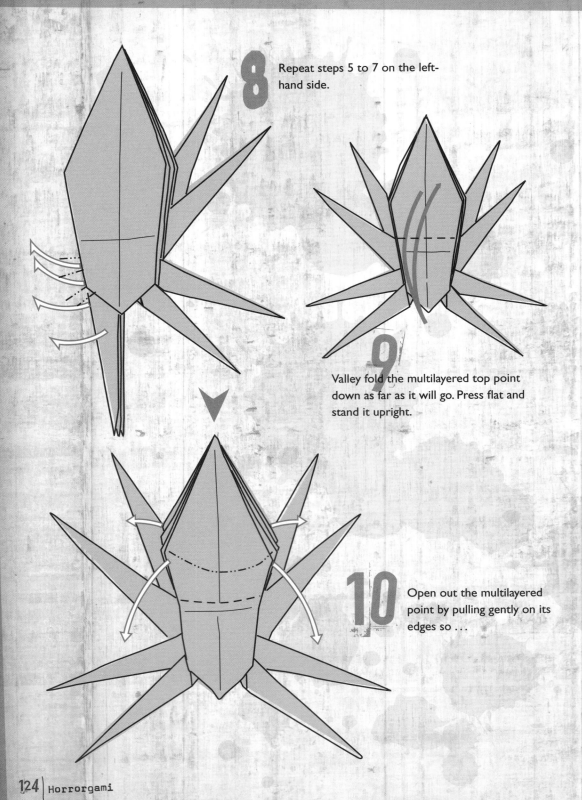

8 Repeat steps 5 to 7 on the left-hand side.

9 Valley fold the multilayered top point down as far as it will go. Press flat and stand it upright.

10 Open out the multilayered point by pulling gently on its edges so ...

11 suggesting the spider's abdomen. To complete the Stupefying Spider, shape its legs with mountain folds as shown.

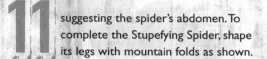

12 If you wish to hang the spider up, turn the model over and attach a length of thread to its rear as shown.

"If you want to live and thrive, let the **spider** run **alive**"
American Quaker Saying

Nice Legs!

Spider's Web

Spider webs are always associated with haunted houses, gothic chapels, and the cupboard under the stairs. Also known as cobwebs, they are one of the most detailed time-consuming natural phenomena that exists, but this one is just for fun.

you will need:
- Square of paper, plain on one side and colored on the other
- Scissors

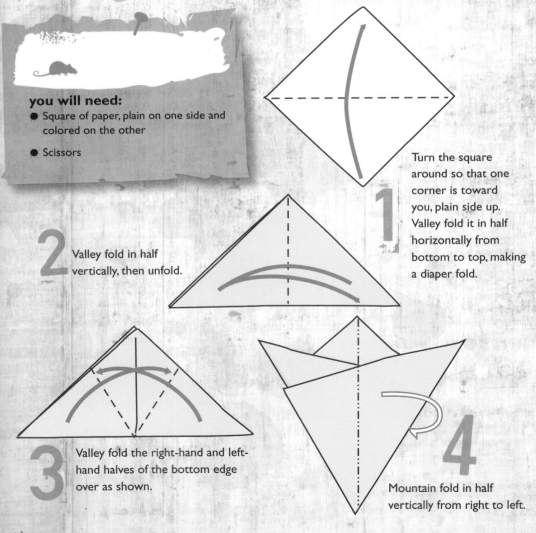

1 Turn the square around so that one corner is toward you, plain side up. Valley fold it in half horizontally from bottom to top, making a diaper fold.

2 Valley fold in half vertically, then unfold.

3 Valley fold the right-hand and left-hand halves of the bottom edge over as shown.

4 Mountain fold in half vertically from right to left.